Remnant Education

Ideas to help you build an independent, post-secondary education in the liberal arts and biblical studies

Raggedy Cottage Garden Independent Publishing

(Self-Published Book May Contain Grammatical Errors)

Unless otherwise indicated, all scripture references are taken from the King James Version of the Holy Bible. The authorized version of the bible holds no copyright.

REMNANT EDUCATION

Copyright © 2016-17 by Laura Spilde

Published by Raggedy Cottage Garden Independent Publishing

www.raggedycottagegarden.blogspot.com

Thank-You to Brandy Williams for editing Remnant Education .

Library of congress information

Printed in United States of America

Romans 11:5

Even so then at this present time also there is a remnant according to the election of grace.

2 Timothy 2:15

Study to shew thyself approved unto God, a workman that needeth not to be ashamed, rightly dividing the word of truth.

Introduction

1. Writing in this book may be like preaching

Some silly ideas are presented, or ideas seem to be exaggerated in this book, but take God's word and study seriously. Don't be a slough when studying herbs, astronomy or musical things. Taking a class called "Obadiah's Understanding of Astronomy" sounds silly, but it is an illustration to encourage greater understanding. Do your best study in such a class. Make sure you are challenged. Many men interpret the bible differently, but the same Lord over all, considers highly the elimination of pride and selfish living. Some highly educated people, believe their education so perfect that they can never fail. This is not truth. Even the most insured man could be seen as a fool if he secretly embezzles money. The most biblical man could fall into the temptation to seek outside advice, if he is not aware of the dangers that actually lurk outside of biblical nourishment and encouragement from biblical friends and family. Education and knowledge that comes from the bible is what enhances and encourages success. The Heavenly Father is a judge. He equips us to understand how to function better as his student, if we are willing to listen to his commandments and his ways.

His ways are higher than our ways. This book is to ensure that knowledge given to us by using our minds in accordance to his word is what enhances and improves the life of humanity.

2. Bible study will be most appetizing to the saved

If you are not a student of the bible on a regular basis, you may not appreciate this book. You may not benefit from it. However, if you are a student of the bible and dive into commentaries, concordances and more bible study tools regularly, this book may be of great benefit to you. It is recommended that a student of the bible use the authorized versions of scripture for their language that they will be using to speak. In English the authorized version of scripture is the KJV Holy Bible. In German or Urdu, it will be the version that is free to the poor and holds no copyright. Consider the date when copyright versions of the bible started arriving in people's hands. Consider the denomination and what bible version that may have inspired the writer.

A saved person wants to know how many times "godly" is mentioned in the bible and wants to memorize those verses as well as a person asks God to help change the person to be more godly. An unsaved person simply doesn't care. They do not take God's word to heart. Even siblings can depart from God's word. Including identical twins! Even parents can choose not to follow scripture. It is all dependant on individual faith!

If a person is persecuted for choosing the bible over the will of their parents, family, government or other issues at hand, that person is doing a good job for the LORD. Mark 3:35 says, "For whosoever shall do

the will of God, the same is my brother, and my sister, and mother."
Keep fighting the good fight of faith. The bible is simply not appetizing
to those outside faith in Christ. A goal in Christianity is to restore all
knowledge to give God the glory!

3. Any denomination or belief of Christianity may use this book

This book is for any and all people that are interested in getting
independent studies in both the liberal arts and in biblical studies. St.
Augustine quoted scripture! I don't know if Constantine quoted
scripture, but I do believe he was big on "changing" Christianity rather
than just leaving it alone for what it is. Yes, his mother was influenced
by Christianity and the scripture. Martin Luther used bible and so too
did Ellen G. White. Even the controversial Calvin used the bible, but this
book doesn't give credit to denomination, it gives credit to "the word"
as some men and women in some denominations didn't say the best of
things in their past, but yet the word was used as a tool to give men
faith and hope. There may even be other denominations that are not
particularly considered Christian that may use this book. I'd rather not
list all the denominations that should or should not use this book.
Lutherans, Mennonite, Presbyterian, Baptist and more could greatly
benefit from this book. It would be a far cry from my use of time to
mention all the denominations developed by Christian beliefs and study
of the bible. Essentially, a protestant may consider this book to be more
valuable than a Catholic and a messianic Jewish person will see more
value in this book than a non-messianic Jewish person. Do not be afraid
to use this book as a Catholic, an independent, an alternative religion or
other person who doesn't necessarily believe that the bible is truly
helpful for all things in life, but can be used for many things in life.
However, if one does follow the "goal" in this book, the "goal" would be
this: to get a college major in studies equivalent to that of a liberal arts

college, but to have the major use of time to be focused on a specific book of the bible which is three chapters or more in length, or a group of several short books that equal three chapters of bible. The other goal of this book is to establish bible study habits, independent study habits, and independent knowledge of skills and focus, clearly and inquisitively on one major book of the bible. When applying for jobs, the student who uses this book will write down that they studied independently and majored in studying "The Book of Job." Most non-Christians will not consider bible study time to be essential use of time and energy. So this book may not be of value to the non-Christian. Hence, Muslims will see college degrees of the book of the bible type to be unessential to their goals in life, which may even be hap hazardous STEM studies to promote terrorism and corruptions in political environments. The goal of this book is to overcome the evil within ungodly men and women's minds in ourselves and in others.

This book is written by a woman author. Do not let that be a distraction to the essential elements and goals of this book. Women are given equal opportunity to express good or evil in this world, just as much as men. Grandmother Lois was godly, Jezebel was wicked. Elijah was godly, King Saul was wicked. Martin Luther King Jr. was a godly man though he had his flaws; Hitler was an ungodly man though he seemed to always be so good. Women are simply the weaker vessel and should focus on preparation for future generations of godly young people and adults. This book is a "plan" and a "goal" to express a more godly vision and give greater liberty to young people, with the release of burden of debt by education. By the age of 20, most young men and young women will come to understand that grandmother Lois (2 Timothy 1) expresses deep desire to teach young Timothy to be godly in knowledge, wisdom and character in whatever way she could teach in the current wicked days. When we see wickedness in our current day, we should not fear, because we who are believers know the scripture.

We know the dimensions of the tabernacle in the wilderness and we know the content of gold, its high price and cost within the valuable tabernacle. Let us use our vessels and tabernacles to be more holy towards our creator.

Dear Heavenly Father,

Lead us by your strong arm to use our time wisely on this earth and be more godly for you in the use of our knowledge and wisdom. May you use us as vessels to change the heart of humanity through the ability of knowledge and wisdom to serve your son Jesus in better ways. In your son Jesus, holy name, Amen.

Table of Contents

Psalms 49:3

My mouth shall speak of wisdom; and the meditation of my heart shall be of understanding.

The Heart is First Seat for Wisdom

The human heart is the seat where humankind meditates on good or evil. If you have encountered people with mental deficiency in life, you will encounter imaginations that have turned towards wicked imaginations. They are willing to distort God's laws and give over to their own. Beliefs become skewed and judgments are altered. Some ignore scripture warnings and some attach themselves to finding cure through the power of the word. No man can gain proper wisdom unless he has attained self-control. A mind filled with envy and anger cannot process and cannot meditate on the precepts of God's word. There is another soul that desires to gain the whole world and loose soul. Such a mind, desires more and more, but he is spiritually dead. Morality is ignored while self will is given dominion. Overcoming selfish intentions is the beginning of wisdom. We don't need more terrorism in this world. Terrorists try to thwart human wisdom and cause calamity on humanity culture and humanity ways of life. Enough is enough. We don't need terrorists to get access to ultimate wisdom. Terrorists and those in other false religious groups will not benefit from true wisdom that comes from God's word. We need people to repent and find true wisdom that comes from God's word first.

In the bible we read in John 7:17, "If any man will do his will, he shall know of the doctrine, whether it be of God, or whether I speak of myself." In this verse, we can see that as followers of Christ we should be followers of how he submitted to the doctrines of God. He submitted to the will of the heavenly father. The Heavenly Father's will was for him to know the bible! Are we willing to submit to the Heavenly Father when it comes to bible study and overall use of our time, money and intellectual talents?

1. The bible is first text book

The first textbook the youth should encounter is the bible. Any other book will not do. It will not supply knowledge about workings of the human heart and how such meditations affect the mind. Language itself is derived from Semitic language; hence the bible holds all definitions necessary to supply man with 'bread of life.' The more the stories of the bible are memorized, the less tempting it becomes for a man to desire to serve himself. The less meditation a man completes in bible study, the more likely he feels non-bible generated writings feed his soul, thus he becomes a man endangered to 'gain the whole world' but lose his soul. A man or woman does not need a large supply of knowledge about the mind and social behaviors to absorb the writings of the bible; he only needs the desire to study scripture from within his heart.

The foolish minds of modern youth believe that the bible ignores function of the human body, thus it is unscientific to the unsaved mind.

This is not truth. The bible mentions the heart, liver, lungs, kidneys on into the hands, eyes, ears and other vital body organs that sustain human and animal life. The adulterated unsaved youths also believe that the bible is not sufficient for social issues such as justice and liberty for people of disability or of different race and nation. Once again, this is not truth as the bible defines its own definitions for justice, mercy, liberty, scorn, derisions, quietness and other gifts from fellowship with Holy Spirit. The bible mentions that people in sin filled places should listen to the bible more, rather than less, Isaiah 1:10, "Hear the word of the LORD, ye rulers of Sodom; give ear unto the law of our God, ye people of Gomorrah." When colleges become Sodom and Gomorrah it is time to cause the student of modern youth to rise up and listen to the LORD.

Furthermore, what about astronomy and advanced science? Is the mind of man capable of learning from an ancient book and absorbing the methods and ways of the calendrical calculations of time such as ancient people used to calculate time and resourcefulness for various processes of time. Yes, a person can learn how the ancient people calculated time, and may even find a way to calculate what the ages of the ancient people meant for fulfilling biblical events. Adam and Noah were clearly more advanced in age and reason than modern man, due to the decaying effect of sin.

Because of the effective resources that arise from biblical account, it is reasonable to eliminate men who hate scripture from all educational processes, specifically the Christian methods of education. A major and study directly from a book of the bible is sufficient to supply the mind and more importantly the heart with effective means of understanding the nature of God and man. An effective major in the book of

'Proverbs,' for example, will supply much needed wisdom for a fully educated man or woman.

2. Nature is second text book

The second textbook for man is nature. Man will encounter all things nature based from the time of his conception, until the day of death. Observance of the ant teaches men to work with his hands diligently and not to be slacking in his labor. Observance and study of the robin will reveal how birds have internal knowledge to build perfectly symmetrical circular nests, and precisely guard the nest of their young. Seeing the lily in the field grow in ditches and in rocky areas reveals that humanity can find itself in harsh places yet grows bright and beautiful and strong despite the surroundings.

Studies of herbal remedy are sufficient to help the mind and heart of man to cure his own clan and nation. Tribes and tongues have survived off of such wisdom since the time of Babylon tower. If one does proper research in Liberal Arts and bible study, conclusions can be made about the change in language made by God and about the original language of the people who built the tower. Did they all speak Greek? Did they all speak a form of Hebrew?

Elimination of faulty and imaginative nonsense in the study of nature is essential. Since the mind and heart cannot time travel, it is not sufficient to study the life of animals that have passed away in the flood or through extinction, and are not with us, and then to spend so much time investigating theories that are not proven truth. It is better to gather seeds of dandelions and learn the natural significance and food supply from the simplest of manna in the wilderness.

Study of astronomy will guide men into eternity. Orders and laws of our universe are guided by patterns which do not change. The first great scientist who formulated ideas about our universe were clearly efficient and diligent students of the bible.

As in all things, our bible gives us a clear picture that the ancient people needed to use nature to develop their supply for living, also there are many ways the bible uses nature to illustrate points and aspects about God. Romans 11:24, "For if thou wert cut out of the olive tree which is wild by nature, and wert graffed contrary to nature into a good olive tree: how much more shall these, which be the natural branches, be graffed into their own olive tree?" In such a verse, nature is used as an illustrator of conditions of the human heart that need dependence on Christ. Perhaps study of the olive tree can exemplify the understanding that goes along with this verse.

3. Possible outline of studies

Nearly everything that men and women study and learn about today can be learned from home and through the filter of scripture to determine the quality of such learning experiences.

The elimination of heartless men who use knowledge for their own selfish glory is essential for the furtherance of the gospel and for the benefit of mankind into the future. Instead of studying only accounting, men and women should study the book of Mathew until each story is memorized and verses of significance are given important value. Classes regarding accounting can be incorporated into the learning process, when stories of 'the tax collector' are mentioned as well as stories about 'feeding five thousand' are mentioned. The more men know and memorize scripture, the less appealing will be the temptation to use knowledge for selfish vain glory.

Anything and everything can be learned and studied. A sufficient college degree will incorporate studies in language (speaking, writing, and communication), music, art, nature, math, history/biblical prophecy, voice, health and so forth. A possible outline of classes for studies based on a major that shows knowledge of a book of the bible can go something like this: Comparisons Between Book of Mathew and Proverbs, Self-Sufficiency Accounting as Examined in the Book of Mathew, The Philosophies of Healing and its Interpretations According to Gospel of Mathew.

Of course, the independent student will design his or her own possible outline of classes. The student can create his or her own course catalogue! No need to describe every detail. Simply list the title of the class, a small paragraph and level of the coursework involved. A sufficient four credit class, will incorporate a greater deal of bible memorization, more pages of various literature read, and will include more challenging tests, quizzes and language and vocabulary expansion.

For the purposes of allowing an example to be expressed, an individual who studies and majors in the book of 'Mathew' will have his senses keened into these types of classes.

Assignment:

1. Create a course catalog. Do not worry if all of the detailed energies and understandings are expressed, rather, incorporate all possible classes that a student may take to complete a 'bible book major.' Include the number of credits desired and a brief paragraph describing topics to be discussed. Separate 'majors' by section of the bible being studied and type of liberal arts study being investigated.

...Law books, Prophets books, Psalms/Proverbs books, Poetry books, Old Testament books, Gospel books, New Testament Books, Revelation Books..... Use a code to indicate type of liberal arts idea being studied(music, arts, nature etc)

2. Outline a possible four year class list that will include all the classes needed for a particular major in the book of the bible.

Note: Completion of this assignment should take about one week or less to complete. Keep careful records of this process. If needed in the process of college study, rent a separate storage space.

3. Study Eden. How were Adam and Eve supposed to care for nature and creation? What is the definition of Eden? What is the definition of Adam and Eve? How are these terms defined in different languages like Greek and Hebrew? How did they fail in their heart? How did they fail in their knowledge? How did they fail in their character? This answer will become more apparent, the more scripture is studied and put into practice.

Quiz:

Evaluate your understanding of what was presented in this selection:

1. What problems exist when people who do not love God get a hold of knowledge and attempt to be in powerful professions?

2. List various ways that the bible is the first text book.

3. List various ways that nature is the second text book for man.

4. What are the various aspects of learning that men and women should study and improve in his or her life?

5. What type of major will the independent bible college student receive?

Proverbs 2:6

For the LORD giveth wisdom: out of his mouth cometh knowledge and understanding.

Creating a Class that will Fulfill Requirements for Knowledge and Wisdom

1. Biblical investigation in knowledge and wisdom

The student who pursues college should do his or her best to incorporate biblical knowledge into his or her curriculum. He should gain so much knowledge that when the trials of life come upon him, he will know what to do in difficult circumstances. What does the bible have to say about wisdom and knowledge?

Proverbs 18:15 states, 'The heart of the prudent getteth knowledge; and the ear of the wise seeketh knowledge.' This verse does not indicate that the man or woman pays for a large college expense to get knowledge. Rather, he or she 'searches' for it. He or she may visit a library regularly and get knowledge through books. Simply writing an outline of each book that is read, will help the person get knowledge! The wise man will seek knowledge, he may perhaps seek for it through asking people from different cultures different questions. He or she may find the ability to discuss hot-topics without forming the belief that he or she stands firmly for or against a certain set of beliefs.

The knowledgeable man in essence does not just 'accept' what his college professor tells him, rather he chooses to do research and search for the answer himself.

2. Adding in sufficient biblical studies into a class

Many secular liberal arts classes do not incorporate biblical advice or questions. In fact, many professors, despise the use of scripture to formulate questions and come up with solutions or answers. Unfortunately, some bible colleges are so severely stuck in the problems that the bible is the only answer to life's issues, that they happen to ignore the reality that people have solved problems in life, before the existence of bible, hence people can become unwise scorners of the wise people in society, thus leading to sin on the biblical college student's part. As the bible verse says in Pro 26:16, "The sluggard is wiser in his own conceit than seven men that can render a reason." Hence, in this verse there is slack and sluggishness from a certain angle in the student. Either it is in the secular man who does not want to use scripture or it is in the pride filled bible studies man who does not want to rely on general reason. One of the two sides considers itself wiser. Essentially, there is an inner battle between the two beliefs. A battle for biblical knowledge as ultimate guide, and a battle to supply general human wisdom and reasoning.

One of the first suggestions is to incorporate specific bible passages for a major into each course syllabus. Each course will require the student to learn and memorize a whole chapter of bible, or investigate certain parts of the bible. Write out a specific objective that allows a student to question how biblical knowledge supplies sufficient resources in the study of philosophical study for example. Each quiz or test, will include testing on the memorization of bible passages as well as the general knowledge presented in books or literature that was used in learning. No test or paper will leave out biblical knowledge as a resource. Perhaps in one test, the student is asked to fully outline a few chapters of bible as well as answer questions about the difference between modern psychology and the book of Proverbs. In another class, the student is asked to compare modern Jewish practices, with modern culture practices of the Native Americans, while explaining how the bible incorporates a unique biblical calendar structure that outlines culture and social events.

Essentially, a class will be sufficient in generating biblical and secular knowledge if it focuses on bible as the theme for generating questions. No biology lesson will eliminate bible, because bible passages about eagles, cypress trees and more will be incorporated.

3. Incorporating secular knowledge

Occasionally, Christians become lazy and unwise. They assume that people who have secular knowledge are always supportive of perversions in the spirit. This isn't the case. In fact, people who enjoy the study of George Washington and antiques are less likely to choose to become a thief or to choose to embezzle church money. Knowing things actually causes people to become humbled, due to the weight of knowledge about the deceitful behaviors of men. This is simply because they are willing to acknowledge that they still do not know all that there is to learn and simply choose more simplistic lifestyles. However, some people become so full of knowledge about the expansions of the universe, that they become religious zealots for religious values that suppress Christian beliefs. All wisdom is good, especially when one recognizes the problems of sin. Pro 10:1 states, " The proverbs of Solomon. A wise son maketh a glad father: but a foolish son is the heaviness of his mother." In the foolish son anger becomes their theme as they know not the savior! They recognize not the importance of repentance before a mighty creator. They may even suppress themselves so much, even with such wisdom about various cultures that they wish not to live any longer and seek the escape route of bondage.

How can one incorporate secular knowledge, without praising it? A course syllabus, of course should be a challenge to the student, enlightening the student with new vocabulary, new ways of doing regular everyday activity, and new ways of calculating how the earth spins on its axis. To incorporate the general secular text into the mind of the learner, basically, a rule of nature should be allowed. Allow the length and number of pages to read and study to be sufficient for the advanced level of the class. A class in astronomy can incorporate general secular concepts, labs, experiments, paper writings and more, but such a class, will also sufficiently supply biblical concepts related to astronomy. Mere mentioning a bible verse or two will not allow the student to incorporate sufficient bible. Instead, the bible passages need to challenge the student to seek ways of understanding the universe, through the lenses of scripture as a means of balancing the orders of nature. Each class in secular knowledge will also include a peek into specific biblical passages that relate to the theme and relate to the vocabularies presented. Overall, the class should be challenging enough for an independent student, that he or she completes a class that is equivalent to the accreditation practice of typical colleges in America and abroad. Yes, secular knowledge could be very unbiblical in its themes and rejection natured towards God as savior and redeemer, especially when studies of genocide or cult practices are incorporated, but gaining wisdom about these things and themes is important to a Christian's life in order to serve humanity and family better.

4. Creating sufficient questions and concepts.

If a student never went to college before, he may need to check out some books about how professors teach. A book or two about how professors, can more effectively encourage their students to learn new concepts, will be very helpful for the independent student. Simply outlining a textbook is only sufficient for a student who does not take his studies seriously. Ensure that each class has a theme or goal in mind. Do not just plan syllabi at random and never seek ways to incorporate biblical knowledge or to avoid secular knowledge and themes. Rather, have themes available to incorporate a bible story into the study of accounting. Incorporate the nature and design of the lily flower, with its six petals and bible passages about the number 'six' with mathematical models (Resources: Numerical Calculations). Each question does not need to incorporate a biblical theme or advice, but each question should allow the student to improve learning equivalently in secular knowledge and in biblical knowledge.

Many different questions are asked through college. The entire theme of college is to ask. To ask, causes a student to search for answers. To know the answers is to have knowledge. Hence, college starts with asking. The best way to develop questions useful for college class, is to generate a list of possible questions. Questions can be in a variety of themes and styles. Questions can be based on a verse like this: Isa 7:15, "Butter and honey shall he eat, that he may know to refuse the evil, and choose the good." Are you able to ask questions that weed out the bad ideas in men and women? Asking questions that point to the reality of the father's saving power, will have everlasting impact on this earth. They could be a general fact question. A hot topic question. A question that generates discussion, questions that reflect the effectiveness of previous learning experiences, and so forth.

5. Quizzes, Projects, Tests, Term Papers

A quiz is a mini test that a student takes once a week or every two class periods. Quizzes typically only cover about ten to twenty questions and do not take an entire class period to complete. The quiz should incorporate vocabulary learned, an outline or paraphrase about a book, biblical themes presented, research goals and more. They can be true false, multiple choice, fill in the blank, discussion questions, paraphrases, and more. Because the independent student may know the answer, if he or she designs his or her own quiz, it is best to create the quiz, well in advance of actual study. Create quizzes off of phrases in text books, while making the syllabi, so that the syllabi will reflect themes in quizzes. Projects, Tests and Term Papers are also developed in this manner.

Assignment:

1. Create effective classes for one full year of study. A typical student can only handle between 12 and 16 credits of course study per semester. Create syllabi of the information that will guide studies for each time classes take place. If needed, check out books from a local library or a college library that describe how professors create their classes.

2. Create a supply list of questions. Check out a book from the library that teaches professors and teachers how to teach more effectively. Create a supply list of questions that can be asked in tests, quizzes, for mini papers, discussion questions and in long term papers. These questions can be simple example questions: How does the story about John the Baptist relate to the problems of divorce and remarriage issues today? What problems in the social work book "X", show the ineffectiveness of fatherless homes?

Quiz:

Evaluate your understanding of what was happening in this selection:

1. Why should biblical knowledge be incorporated into secular studies?

2. What verse illustrates that men who focus only on either bible studies or secular studies become "wiser" in a conceit filled way?

3. What should be developed to help an independent student overcome the burden of not knowing what will be studied?

4. What is the theme of college which causes students to learn more?

5. Name some things that should be included in quizzes, tests and other assignments.

1Thessalonians 4:11

And that ye study to be quiet, and to do your own business, and to work with your own hands, as we commanded you;

The Habit of Bible Study

1. Study scripture five times a day

Have you ever tried to read a piece of literature several times through each day? Practicing for a part in a play requires a person to recite phrases, verses and lines several times a day.   One must be familiar with the whole picture of the play in order to do a good job in the role you have been asked to do in the play. If a person only reads one verse a day, that person will not play a big part in the play, but will be more like the person on the side, perhaps just a person among the crowd.   A person who plays a big role in the production will be a person who is fully familiar with the script and has several lines memorized.   To enhance this, study is essential for the bible college student. They must not and may not just be enhanced by common cultural verses, but with deep internal verses that actually hold a solid foundation in the faith. These verses help explain why the condition of kindness is expressed among Christians much more readily than among unbelievers. In Psalm 119 it is mentioned that the worshiper actually worships seven times a day! Psalm 119:164 states, "Seven times a day do I praise thee because of thy righteous judgments." Perhaps one can conclude that each worship session involved a little something different each time in order to stimulate such worship.

An invitation to worship is presented in the scripture. Seven times a day is this invitation presented. When the sun goes down in the evening, a plan is put in place to continue worship for the entirety of the day. In the evening, perhaps the student studies astronomy and how it coordinates with scripture. Study the relation of planets, stars, moons, galaxies in our solar system. Such study would be interesting to the worshiper. Not only that, but consider the condition of the morning glory, or nocturnal animals in evening hours after the sun has set.

In the morning, after rest, the student wakes up at a sufficient time and begins bible study. Psalms and proverbs can be studied. Meditation brings healing to the soul and awareness of the mind to coordinate with the divine. The psalms and proverbs are a book of enhancement to modern day, and historical issues relating to sociology and psychology. One can reflect on five psalms and one proverb a day depending on the day of the month. Write down verses that coordinate with current studies or with other issues important to the student.

Before lunch is prepared a student can choose quality hymns to practice and memorize. Or practice prayers for others. Anything that allows the student to eliminate unwanted anxieties and interruptions on the process of worship towards Christ.

Immediately during the lunch hour, the student can study the law or torah portions of scripture. Awareness of God's law and studies of patriarchs, assists the student in understanding the divine nature of

Christ. A couple of chapters in the first five books can be read in parashah style. These chapters can be studied thoroughly throughout one week (more information in Resources). Emphasis on the story as well as emphasis on the comprehension of each verse should be studied. Pay attention to verses and concepts regarding character. Knowledge of the law portion of the bible will help the student stand strong in a world of confusing ideas that belittle the importance of God's word. Also, knowledge of the law portion of the bible will help the bible student understand the remaining bible, on into the New Testament and book of Revelation.

Following the lunch hour and into the afternoon, the bible study student should incorporate study of the Old Testament passages that do not include the Psalms, Proverbs and the law. This would include any books like Judges, Song of Solomon and Nehemiah. About 9-10 chapters should be included in this study per week. One or two chapters can be studied during one day. Like the law portion, focus on comprehension, memorization of verses and character issues presented. The verses and ideas can be used within the secular liberal arts studies to emphasize the importance of scripture knowledge to enhance such arts and science program of study.

Before the evening meal, and perhaps towards sun down in the wintertime months, the bible study student should study the gospels. He or she should study Matthew, Mark, Luke and John. In a basic liberal arts Christian college, the teacher in religion will emphasize the sameness of the story among the gospels, and attempt to persuade the student that the verses were copied, while minimizing the actual assistance in the scripture at understanding Christ as redeemer of mankind. These types of teachings attempt to distract the student from enjoyment of diligent gospel study. A selection of two chapters in one of the books can be studied. The student may coordinate the passages with other portions of the bible, and determine how the issue presented in the bible also relates to today's dilemmas. As well as to the bible directly.

After the sun has set and evening hours are at hand, it is good to study New Testament passages. Study about three chapters per week. Re-read important verses and memorize verses that really enhance the necessity of the gospel. Absorb these verses in song. Make them interesting and fulfilling to the student. The more a student knows about the New Testament, the less appealing will be the conditions of our current world.

Of course, in between these times of study, be sure to visit strangers, widows and orphans by singing, teaching and provision of food shelter and clothing.

2. Ways to incorporate study

How may an individual incorporate actual bible studies into a basic lesson involving only art, music or nature study. Simple. One can choose educational materials which specifically point out the truths of scripture as reliable for reproof and correction, or one can summarize the information presented in a secular manner, but use the current bible studies material for the week, within the context of secular study.

2 Ti 3:16 states, "All scripture is given by inspiration of God, and is profitable for doctrine, for reproof, for correction, for instruction in righteousness." The bible is given for correction even of secular knowledge to bring righteousness to this earth! If one is studying biology, for example, a student can eliminate the studies of evolution and discern actual biblical references in these matters. Or, if one is studying psychology, a person can find the flaws and errors in psychologist thought vs. actual biblical psychology behavior as referenced in the current Psalms and Proverbs study.

As the goal of a bible college liberal arts student is not to have all knowledge either in bible or in liberal arts alone, each class will consist of the chapters associated with the major of choice. Memorization of verses will take place, in relation to the chosen major. Do not make the classes so simplistic, that no thought is given to the value of the bible in the studies. Rather, be sure to include specific memory and study of the scripture along with the secular art book assigned. Quizzes will include one chapter or two that were referenced in the bible according to the chosen student's major as well as quizzing the knowledge of the secular text. Perhaps the student studies Beethoven, so the student will have a quiz involving the relationship between the thoughts presented in the bible, memorization of verses, knowledge about the topic of Beethoven and questions comparing the necessity for knowledge in each of the areas of study.

Perhaps if the class involves learning skills, such as carpentry, etiquette and fine dining, the student may incorporate stories from the bible about such situations, verses which refer to either scorn or kindness and practical life experience about these matters. The bible study liberal arts student should still seek to enhance study of a specific book of the bible into the current studies, even if the class happens to be a skill or project based study.

3. No need for classes to 'study' bible, but habits are effective directors

If one would like to incorporate a 'bible quiz' class, or an introduction to the bible, the student would be wise in including such a thing. Pro 15:10 states, "Correction is grievous unto him that forsaketh the way: and he that hateth reproof shall die." Corrections in knowledge are important for both the liberal arts student and the bible studies student. Without such a class, all the knowledge of religion would not be available to the student and the student would wander around, assuming all religions are equal. The reality is that religions differ, one from another. There are other aspects of history, that the bible study student may overlook due to excessive religious training in a conservative view as well, so such an overview of the bible class, can assist the liberal arts bible study student. With the basic understanding of the bible in check, then the entire bible becomes easier to grasp in understanding.

There may be classes in a bible college which specifically study the law portions of the scripture, the proverbs or other specific book of the bible, but essentially these classes are only necessary if they relate to study of the students major, which would be a book of the bible. Rather, the liberal arts bible college student will study various arts and sciences to enhance his or her strengths in wisdom and knowledge in various areas as well as enhancing knowledge of the scripture. When the student becomes used to this approach of study a 'habit' becomes a part of the students life. They no longer feel that they will wander in thoughts with no reflective moral direction. Rather, they will form the habit of consulting scripture to enhance study. Each class will include at least one chapter per class in study of the students major as it relates to the study at hand. Forming the habit of including bible in the studies as well as developing more skills in various arts and sciences, will fully equip the student to undertake any and all pressures of life that may come in the student's direction. Forming the habit of study in the scripture at various degrees and levels and in various parts, also helps the student to develop habit to consult the scriptures, regularly throughout the day, rather than turning aside to fictitious literatures, media and other faulty forms of entertainment which degrade and dilute the soul with evils.

A habit formed in a young student of sixteen will be a habit established in the student at sixty five years of age.

Assignment:

1. Practice study of the bible five times a day. If you normally read about three chapters a day, improving your bible study habits to include reading bible five times a day will make you more aware of the various lies, manipulations and other poor habits that have invaded your life and the lives of others.

2. Create a possible quiz in a book of the bible. Create this quiz combining the knowledge of an art with the book of the bible. This quiz should show that the student studied the art as well as incorporated knowledge about a book of the bible.

Quiz:

Evaluate your understanding of what was presented in this selection:

1. What time of the day is it suggested that a person study Psalms and Proverbs?

2. How may a person read Psalms and Proverbs according to the day of the month and according to the pattern?

3. If a person is learning how to sew a quilt, would that person still need to incorporate bible studies into the skill and class?

4. If a student has a paper assigned that asks to explain the events of Abe Lincoln's life while being born in Nebraska and also the details of the book of Hezekiah, explain why knowledge in details of the bible as well as details in secular studies helps eliminate false ideas.

5. If a class asks to explain what miracles the Egyptian magicians could not perform while studying secular chemistry, how can the study of both bible and secular knowledge help eliminate various lies humanity commonly encounters?

Daniel 1:4

Children in whom was no blemish, but well favoured, and skilful in all wisdom, and cunning in knowledge, and understanding science, and such as had ability in them to stand in the king's palace, and whom they might teach the learning and the tongue of the Chaldeans.

Ways to Incorporate the Arts

1. Natural Sciences

First, choose a liberal arts college manual. Go through the manual and find all the natural science classes. Classes like Biology I and II. Classes about physics and astronomy. Imagine possible texts that may be used in these particular college classes. Perhaps one big text book and one lab manual. Take note on the number of credits the class is worth. When study of biology occurs, set aside a little time to perform a lab. In some biology classes, the lab is worth 1 credit and the class it-self is worth three credits. Of course, a student may choose not to use lab equipment or the student may choose to use lab equipment. Equipment like microscopes, Petri-dishes may need to be purchased in addition. Is there a lab-manual that can be used in conjunction to the class? Search internet and libraries for lab manuals. The lab manual does not need to match the textbook material exactly. Rather, it is best to simply complete lab procedures as needed. What if the class involves physics. There again, be sure to incorporate labs on lights, energy and so forth that would help amplify the concepts learned.

Select the textbook that would be used. Yes, it is easier to use a basic textbook as the titles, subtitles, vocabulary and questions are all pre-arranged for you. In fact, it doesn't have to be "Christian" textbook. It is also optional to include a specific website, videos and supplemental material that will help in understanding the concepts presented. One can simply understand that it is not Christian or biblically based text and then either eliminate the parts about "evolution" or a student can incorporate the current biblical study to examine why "evolution" doesn't work and what parts are not apologetically accurate, for example. Definitely do a thorough study on inaccuracies and a complete study on the value of knowing different aspects about the particular natural science. Do not be slough like and ignore identification of trees, simply because you never did that before. No, make sure to include new concepts. Perhaps your particular class is entitled "Entomology in Comparison to the Book of Genesis and Job." Such a class should include many principles that enhance knowledge in both bible and in Entomology.

2. Musical Notations

There are lots of classical music in the liberal arts college library. There are also lots of pianos, tubas and other unusual instruments. A harpsichord and old pipe organ can be found at a liberal arts college. This makes going to a liberal arts college so appealing. It is because the student does not need to search high and low for a chance to play a harpsichord and can get together with a group of students to string out some fine classic tunes on a cello. However, such appeal to "the flesh" can actually drain the human spirit in the long run. Read the psalms several times through in the bible and you will start to grasp this disproportional appeal to the flesh vs. the actual human spirit. Focus so heavily on music is good to help master. Mozart and many of the early classic musical composers were writing and playing music like professionals before they reached the age of 12. They simply didn't have anything else to do. Except if they were poor and always had to carry firewood to grandpa and grandma.

The question one should simply ask is this. Do you really need to go to a liberal arts college to learn how to improve your musical skills? Ear training and knowing how to hum the right note without hearing the note before is essential if you want to be a good musician. When creating a musical based class, be sure to include biblical concepts as well. Perhaps highlight the various verses that mention music. Does the bible specifically mention that "Christian Rock" music just doesn't seem to flow together right in the same sentence? That is like saying "Christian fornication" is normal. Perhaps, one needs to look deeper at the lifestyle of the classical composers. Some did not practice very pure marriages or have pure relationships, yet they were able to strum out some beautiful classical works.

To improve one's skill in piano, it is good to have comparison to a more skilled piano player. One can tune into the various free classical music available on the internet. Listen to the tune and ensure that your skill is equal to the skill presented by a professional piano player. Can you improve your skill so much that you can devise your own classical CD? In some ways, it appears that the place where you will find the most appeal to improve musical skill, particularly classical music skill is predominately in a liberal arts college. However, this does not mean that this is where most of your emphasis in your life should go. Yes, perhaps you can independently master musical values without getting an entire music degree. But why pay such a high price, when you can do so with independent study. I am sure, the professional orchestras are simply looking for a quality musician. They are looking for a person with knowledge in various areas of music and skill. They are not looking at your spirituality. Even in the Nazi era of WWII, so much appeal to the flesh was more of an emphasis than to the spirit, and as a result, people actually died because people simply didn't care.

Definitely improve your ability to sing mightily to the Lord in Psalms and hymns. These values will have the most light in eternity! Would you like to improve your musical skills, without attendance at a college? Perhaps you may write an ad in a paper and ask anyone if they are interested in developing a musical group that particularly sings hymns or plays classical music of some sort. Ensure that you inform them that you are interested in biblical studies and are not interested in folly entertainment which includes alcohol of sorts along with musical practice.

If you include a class entitled, "Hymn Composition Based on the Book of Mathew," your class structure will be wisely arranged. Classes may also include essentials necessary to the "music major," but yet incorporate biblical concepts. "Ear Training and Theory Arrangement with Genesis." Such a class would look for musical values and concepts listed in Genesis and study those concepts as well as general musical improvement classes.

3. Speaking Effectively

The way we speak can equate to the power of our character. Is your character good? Your voice will show it. Is your character bad? Your voice will show it. Do you lack wisdom. There again, your words and conduct will show when you lack wisdom? Great speeches by great men of character in the past are written down. Then again, great humble men who have never had a their words published before the eyes of worldly men, have had their speeches muffled by the voices of this world, yet we definitely need such strength in humility.

A class that builds confidence in speech, particularly speech while reading from the bible is a very good class to have. What would it be like to watch a movie and only to hear the actors speak in a dull tone? It would not be a very good movie. Does a dull voice equal a morally corrupt man? Maybe it could be the case, and maybe it could not be the case. It will depend. High dramatic voices, draw people to new ideas in the scripture, never before presented. But so much appeal to entertainment in the voice, reveals a lack of dignity and respect for the holy scripture.

Can language be improved by bible study? Definitely. Wisdom is gained by bible study. Where would the words of Abe Lincoln and Martin Luther King Jr. have come, without the aid of scripture? Those words would not even exist without such a heart for biblical world view!

A quality language improvement class would perhaps include biblical concepts as well as general language improvement. A class entitled, "Speeches of Past Great Men from Biblical Prophets to Modern Man" Another class that improves speeches could be, "Linguistic Improvement and Appeal According to the Book of Obadiah." An example of a modern man that speaks to people of our time is Benjamin Netanyahu. Though he doesn't appeal to the general Christian belief, he appeals to the original Judeo man in his speeches and emphasis for improvement in the moral condition of humanity. A man with great speech ability, does not need to be a politician. Such battles are not always sane. The far-left, believes things beyond the reality of human and animal life. No, great speeches can be done on a community stage before a community gathering. In the internet age, speeches about humanity issues can be done through internet, as necessary to supply the human spirit with necessary truths.

How can one improve speech, without driving a wedge to appeal to political devices? It will entirely depend on the relationship man or woman has to the holy spirit. Essentially, a person's voice should be clean and humble enough that he or she does not sound too proud even if the person is asked and able to work at a simple bakery.

4. Historical Knowledge

To gain a degree from a book of the bible, the student should have a good background in historical knowledge. A class should focus on biblical understanding surrounding the specific historical aspect. For example, study the events in WWII, but tie in the feelings of the people in that time by referencing Psalms and Proverbs. Any aspect of history can work by referencing the book of the bible along with the historical event. Any culture can be referenced as well. For example, Montezuma can be studied along with biblical reference on the feeling of the people surrounding the historical event. An individual that is well versed in psalms and proverbs will have clearer understanding of why historical events are negative and why the historical events are positive at any given time. Perhaps an individual can create a class entitled "Trail of Tears and Events in the Life of Cherokee in Relation to the Book of Jeremiah." So difficult questions can be asked which can be answered as well with biblical knowledge and historical knowledge.

5. The Cliff Hangers - Religion and philosophy

Does a person need to know all the pillars of Islam to understand the negative effects of this religion? No, not really. Muhammad was not pure in his lifestyle. Does a person need to study Orthodox Judaism to the point of disbelieving the bible and New Testament and returning to Orthodox ways? No, not really. Does a person need to go to every Hindu person to understand the religious experience of Hinduism? No, not really. Rather, when studying a specific religious topic, always include a biblical focal point as well. Comparisons of the book "Song of Songs" with the treatment of women within a specific religion can give quite an illustration of woman's rights as restricted by some religious practices.

One can find benefits towards Christian beliefs from different religions some times as well. For example, Native American religious beliefs are to be humble, honor elders and avoid gaining much possession. Focus on character improvement is group based, not individual based.

Study of Philosophy can throw a person through a loop of conversational changes and choices. Should we avoid such classes, because they require the person to "change" the thinking? It is dependent on what a person can handle really. Does a person want to ride a Ferris wheel or not at the Ferris fair? It would be the same with philosophy. In fact, the early philosophers actually did reference the bible Old Testament in coming up with their ideas about how the mind and spirit work together. To ignore classical works, is to remain in the dark cave. To come to be aware of the changes in people's thinking and how this affects their religious life, is to know what to do when people are choosing to make incorrect beliefs about others or about themselves. Perhaps a couple of classes could be entitled "Classical African Religions as Compared to the Book of Exodus" or "Practices of Character in Classical Philosophy in Comparison to Psalms and Proverbs." Ensuring the student has a solid foundation in knowledge, would ensure that the student is not afraid of different aspects of religion and philosophy.

6. Culture and Social work

Cultures change shift and grow around the world. Even Judaism has changes and shifts. But the word remains the same. Unchanged. It would make a person more aware of life outside of their own culture and hometown to read works and get to know people of a different culture and lifestyle. One may use a textbook to guide through the specific culture, though talking to real people from that specific culture, is what benefits humanity. Reading raw books from actual people from that culture will give a true love for that specific community. Is that culture endangered with religious violence? Does that culture lack gospel? These things may also be asked.

Perhaps, you would like to use your specific biblical knowledge to bring the gospel to those people. Ensure you have enough knowledge of the bible as well as a social understanding of how the gospel transformed people's lives in the past and can transform it for the future. However, be aware that gospel itself never destroys culture. Any time it does that, impure religious value has been imposed on the people. This is not truth and love in humility. Rather it is a destructive force of pride against the soul and heart.

In the study of culture, be sure to include a study of a book of the bible. "An Exodus from the World Among the Sami" could be a possible title for a class. Be sure to understand how "Culture Shock" can affect people by the forcing of change in their culture or other aspects of moving from place to place around the world.

7. An Art Filled Basket

Many people find enjoyment in hobby. Particularly hobby that involves turning items from nature into something useful for everyday life. Could a class include "Ancient Basketry and Stories from Old Testament" or something of that nature? Perhaps one could study pottery and start up a mini pottery store, with the idea in mind to keep the book of Jeremiah in mind. The more art knowledge one has in mind, the better the ability of the person to survive social dilemmas. Of course, when one has biblical knowledge and art knowledge, immoral art will not be seen as valuable to the eye. Immoral art that promotes debauchery will be seen as distasteful.

Some people even go so far as avoiding the images of "Jesus." Yes, it can be researched that the image of Jesus should not be in the form of a picture image, but should be in the form of bible reading and meditation. That is the clearest picture of Jesus one will ever really get! The picture of Jesus that people may see, can actually be a picture of a counterfeit historical figure who promoted gross immorality contrary to God's laws.

Consider drawing nature pictures. The images we see of nature are all around us. Nature will be with us as long as we are alive. Drawing birds, nests, flowers and trees can help a person become more aware of the inner details of nature around us. Painting the flower, can help us become aware of the need for such colors in our lives. Finding the patterns on the inner working sunflower, can allow the individual to see the power of patterns in creating works of life.

Recycled art. Use boxes, cereal containers, water bottles, plastic bags and more to create more and more quality items for the home and office. Yarn can be added to a bleach bottle container to make a wonderful basket. Old foam trays can be turned into stamping materials. Eggs that are close to the expiration date can be used as paint by simply adding a few drops of food coloring to the yolk. Old blocks of wood may also be used to create toys and other items for the home.

Art that Orthodox Jewish woman create is very interesting. If you do some internet research, you will find art made by Orthodox Jewish woman. Getting familiar with the holidays of the bible and the holidays of the orthodox Jewish people, can help you understand two worlds better. Their world and your need to know the bible better. Purim is not commonly celebrated by the gentile world, but it definitely means a lot to the Jewish people! Other holidays mean a lot to them too. Passover and Sukkot or Feast of Tabernacles. Do your research on these crafts and you will find much information about biblical holidays.

Native American art and nature art are useful. Pine needles can be used to make baskets. So too, may grasses be woven to make rugs. The leather of a deer hide may be used to make clothing. Nature is with us. Do we respect it? Do we use it to build up our culture and our homes to make them more loving? Some Native Americans love to draw and paint images of themselves, such as a horse and rider. These types of art may also be considered, but I would definitely focus more deeply on needed items for the home and useful tools for everyday life. Cat-tail and its many uses should definitely be considered when creating native American types of art. What type of class would you call a Native American art class? Perhaps the name of the class may be called something unusual "Lunar art of the Native American Tribe and Biblical Calendar Studies" or "Ezekiel's Words Similarities in Native American Art and Supply"

Bible Story Art. Here, portions of the bible may be used to illustrate the need for more bible study. The art may be as detailed as that found in an Egermeier story book. Or the art may be as simple as a line drawing that illustrates the thunder and lightning upon Mt. Sinai, as God gave the commandments. Need to focus on character, such as cleanliness, perseverance, godliness, wisdom and more aspects may be illustrated with bible story art. Portray the nature image and the actions of the people in such art. A good class could be called, "Bible Stories of Exodus Illustrating God's Laws." Such a class could include focus on Exodus and allowing the student to study and practice different art forms from pottery to pencil drawing and recycled materials, to illustrate the need to focus on God's laws.

8. Skills Galore

Electrician skills, plumbing skills, off-the-grid skills, media skills, blogging and internet skills, cooking, sewing and cleaning skills. You name it. Skills are needed. Health and healing skills are also a part of life. Consider those skills. Do you need to attend a little community college to help develop and improve those skills? Perhaps that may be helpful. If the skill is encouraging debauchery or something ungodly, like how to serve liquor to 1000 people in one day or how to hunt down a police officer and create social unrest, such a skill is never needed by a godly man or woman. Other basic necessity skills will always be needed. When learning the skill, through a textbook or through a college class, consider adding in the study of a specific book of the bible as well.

Focus on the "character" aspects of the book of the bible. Is wisdom needed according to the bible verses? Consider that when learning the skill. Create a class called, "Study of Electrical Household Wiring and Meditations from Book of Romans." If the class happens to come from a local community college, perhaps a focal point in the study can be a specific book of the bible as an addition to the class, without specifically informing the teacher of such an additional study.

In some cases, skills may be necessary, but some practices that people do in those skills are not entirely safe for humanity, or the skill may have selfish motives attached to the skill. Certain ethical considerations should be applied to skills like health based skills or education based skills for example. Perhaps the class could be entitled "Book of Genesis in Beginning and Ending of Overall Human Health." In such a class, consider multiple aspects of culture that affect human health choices, herbal remedy vs. pharmaceutical cures and so forth. What about midwifery in the book of Genesis and its use in the modern day? Such a class could include herbal remedy methods as well as basic CNA skills to assist with bedside assistance.

9. Math, Accounting, Economics

There is a good way to use math, accounting and economics. And there is an evil way to use math, accounting and economics. When we who follow the Lord and follow bible teachings understand the difference between the good and the evil, we will be less drawn to that which is evil. Math can be used to prepare land for a garden. Math may also be used to justify that a certain vaccine is "working" while in most cases it is failing the human life. Distorted statistics, skews man's understanding of how to survive as it is flavored with political agendas. Godliness with contentment is great gain. Being content with what we already have, is of great value. Being discontent, says we are not aware of the evil in our hearts that can brew. Use math, accounting and economics to be content. A woman should be content with the number of children she has been given and the possibility for many children by the LORD, especially if she has not been enslaved by a government or other force which take the child away from her.

Many people do not like math. However, without math we would not know that smoking causes certain diseases. We would not know what time the sun rises and how the universe functions. We would not want to count how many verses of the bible we have memorized or how many times we have covered those verses. Learning math can be difficult for some people. Because of this, it is best to focus on basic math. Basic math involves these math functions: numeration (counting), addition, subtraction, multiplication, division. These are the basic functions of all math. There is a way to develop more godly understanding of math. Look through the bible and find cases were math is mentioned. Numbers 0-12 have mentioning in the scripture! Find verses relating to "nothing." Find verses relating to "one." Continue on up to 12. Even find verses that mention a multiple of another number. For example, if a bible verse mentions "25 cubits," one can reduce the number to be a multiple of "5." Finding these biblical patterns helps our understanding of math from a godly perspective. Furthermore, look into nature as well. Find things in nature that represent 0-12. How many petals are on a flower? How many veins are positioned on a leaf? How many legs are on a critter? Such patterns in nature are all around us and will not leave us as long as we are on this earth. Certainly, one may dive into deeper mathematical principles such as the Fibonacci formula which revolves around the number "seven" and as God finished his work in "seven days." Furthermore, God himself chose Jesus to be born into a family that was simply a carpenter's family. So look deeply into these things. Not only that, but Noah definitely had some superior engineering skills to build such an ark. Perhaps a good name for a math class with biblical foundations could be "Vector Calculus in Agreement to the Book of Genesis."

To make note of the changes and alterations to scripture as Satan himself has tried to manipulate, one will need a good solid understanding of mathematics and reasoning. Knowing the biblical mathematical construction will help greatly. In the KJV English bible, one will find repetitions of certain sounds, vs. elimination of other sounds. "Sc" sound is only mentioned a certain number of times in the bible and each time it will be only a certain set of words with "sc" sound. It will not include all the "sc" sounding words in the English language. Also, the Qumran calendar was hidden for many centuries. No one can establish the understanding that scripture is in fact for yesterday, today and tomorrow, because man cannot understand how the bible calendar works accordingly as answered in Genesis. Planets, stars, moon phases and patterns of the moon all account to the glory of God and redemption through Christ alone. To study these things, consider resources by Gail Riplinger, www.sonlighteducation.com and www.kingscalendar.com by R.P. Ben BenDedeck.

Accounting is good for establishing responsibility. Do not try to avoid accounting, simply because you hate to keep track of details. Noah needed to keep track of his supply and demand for supply in order to function despite living in a wicked world. Know the vocabulary terms of accounting, will help you improve in your ability to know what is going on in your accounts. Jesus used tax collectors as reference to them as being more potential for heaven as well as a close disciple. If you are not good at accounting, consider studying the frugal lifestyle. How have people managed to live during hard times? If you are good at accounting, consider helping the poor meet their needs. Accounting should be done in a way that good is established in the earth and not evil. Thinking responsibly and diligently in accounting will help people strive for more godliness. So too, with accounting that has good principles, there may be an embezzler or a Judas that tries to manipulate. Others may try to use political gambles to prove one power as good over the other, when in fact only Christ is good. A good class in accounting would definitely consider the book of Proverbs. Perhaps a good class could be entitled "Accounting in Accord with the Book of Proverbs."

Finally, like math and accounting, economics has good and bad principles to apply. Knowing terms and phrases can help understand why banks fail and why they survive in hard times. Knowing how to be prepared when evil starts to manipulate itself in the earth can help the bible believer greatly. A good class in economics may be entitled, "The Book of Revelation and the Economic Conditions of our World."

10. Other Languages

Knowing other languages helps you to understand other people. You will be less likely to falsely judge people if you know their language! The Native American languages are not Latin based languages. Perhaps you should try to learn why the culture of Native American people is not the same as European or African cultures. Learning Hebrew can actually help you develop an attraction to the bible and to the people who wrote the bible. Right in Psalm 119 we find the Hebrew language as title for the divisions of the chapter. Knowing that meditation is commonly practiced by Jewish people in Old Testament torah can help one understand why the word is powerful and sharper than two edged sword. Satan does not like people who know his word and meditate on it. Whether it is in English or in Hebrew.

Other Latin based languages may also be learned. Spanish, French and Latin are a few languages that one could use if they wish to dwell in different countries outside of the United States. Perhaps you could go so far as translating the bible into a language that does not yet have the full bible translated for them! There are still languages that the Indigenous Americans speak today that do not have a bible in their full language, yet they are forced to learn English and other Latin languages!

One could entitle a language class something like "Hebrew and Translation and Meditation of Psalm 119" or "Translation of the Book of Daniel for Iroquois People Tribe and Tongue." The possibilities are endless. In fact, there are resources which tell us what languages exist in this world since the fall of the tower of Babel. Because we live in end times, the new world order tries to manipulate language and religion to create a universe where Christ didn't die for sin, so definitely be aware of that condition.

11. From my health to yours

Health will not leave you as long as your body is on this earth. If you are following Christ, you will be required to be a "Good Samaritan" to someone somewhere. Healing doesn't start with medicine. Healing starts with God. Doctors who do not follow biblical orders are more likely to make poor ethical choices. Do a bible search on all the major organs of the body from heart, to kidneys to liver. Memorize those verses. The vital organs of the body keep the heart functioning and the life of the person functioning. The more a person knows about diseases that affect humanity, the more likely the person will be able to assist those people in those conditions. Even getting a CNA license will help a general person work with disabled people more effectively. It is not recommended for Christians to get into healthcare unless they are financially aware of the consequences and effect it can have on the home and family life. Many patients around us need help. (Once a spouse has been employed by healthcare, the spouse will not have time for family and attention to the other spouse, hence creating more health and behavior problems in the home.) Also, the social choices of professional healthcare workers can be non-Christian, so do not assume that all healthcare employees are serious about their walk with Christ, even if the hospital is entitled "Christ the King Presbyterian Hospitals."

Natural health has some positive benefits for humanity. It teaches people how to heal themselves and not to worry. Medical insurance is not needed when people choose natural health care methods. Pharmaceutical companies have some manipulative effects as mentioned in scripture under the title pharmakia. Study these negative effects as indicated by pharmakeia! Dietary changes which eliminate sugars and large amounts of meat can significantly reduce the likelihood of earlier death. Furthermore, people who regularly read the bible are less likely to choose alcohol and cigarettes or other harmful substances. Wise people who love biblical diets will even eliminate addictions to unnatural sugar!

Definitely learn different herbs mentioned in the bible and how they heal the body. Also seek to learn herbal remedies used by other cultures including Native American and other tribes around the globe. You will find that "leaves are for the healing of the nations" as found in Revelation is a true statement even for today! Evergreen needles heal the body with high amounts of vitamin "C"!

Mental health can have spiritual and religious causes. Be aware of those things. Do you find that people with mental health problems also avoid bible study and or fellowship with other believers? Do you find that people with mental health problems may have a tendency to choose selfish words and phrases? Look into those issues. Look into the possibility that addictions are caused by not knowing the word. A possible health class could be "Anatomy and Bible Verse Identifications" or "Behavior Issues and the Cure Through the Book of John."

Along with regular health of the body, consider maternity issues. Without maternity, no human being would exist on the earth. The new age movement attempts to distort the purposes and possibility for human life to exist on the earth. In some cases, severe ethical problems happen where the bible is not allowed into homes and villages, simply because governments believe they can control the life of women and the amount of children she can or cannot bring into the world. Unassisted childbirth seems like a new age thing, but study the bible more deeply and one will discover that the Hebrew women were brave enough to overcome the world system of the Egyptians and give birth without medical assistance! Study unassisted childbirth, whether you would choose to use this method of bringing children into the world or not. Study how to be a doula. Such a class created independently in study will benefit your own home and other homes as well. A class entitled "Homebirth and Reflections in Book of Revelation" would be quite an interesting class. Unfortunately due to the possibility of failed pregnancy, the effects of this should also be studied. Disabled children can develop in the womb and choose not to thrive in this world. Knowing how to deal with the issue of pregnancy termination as according to the bible should be highly considered. All things unnatural in the maternity issues also create spiritual turmoil as well, in homes and families.

12. Traditions, Home, Survivability and Sustainability

Some traditions are developed before cultures had access to bible teachings. Does this mean that traditions are bad? No. It simply means that the word itself is what enables humanity to thrive, not religion. The study of traditions that are based on holiday, such as Christmas, should be studied in its positive and negative aspects. Yes, there is pagan history to various traditions. Study and ensure you know these things! The more truth you know, the less likely you will join the crowds and socialize with people in an ungodly sort of way. Even look into how the first immigrants to America sought to eliminate the "Christmas tree" and wanted to study bible alone. Does this mean that all people who put up Christmas tree are bad people? No. Does this mean that all people who have a dream catcher on their window are bad people? No. It simply means that the word itself is truth to save people and traditions are not. A class that would have many conservative biblical principles would be entitled, "Merry Traditions Through Time vs. the Book of Daniel and the Tower of Babel"

Home life is where people will find enjoyment. Without a home, people do not have privacy. Without a place to put bible verses on our walls, our world will corner us with attempts to sell this and that. A home can be small, or it can be large. Knowing how to take care of the home whether it is electrical or non-electrical will give a better life in the long run. There are lots of wonderful books on homemaking written before the 1930's. Even homemaking books up until the 1950's are valuable as they encourage women to keep their home clean first, before venturing out and trying to keep the world clean. When the home is in order, then the world will be a better place. A Native American or tribal woman's home may not be pretty, but when she keeps it neat and tidy, she will be in a happy home. Even good homes are found in campers for some people! Knowing how to build a log cabin home is a wonderful thing to know as well as knowing how to build a cob-home or alternative home can keep people aware of the possibility to live without mortgage debts. What a wonderful class to study if it was entitled, "The Value of Home According to Titus" or "Home Life Lost in the Book of Jeremiah."

Survivability. It is good for a family to know how to survive. Not only in the middle of a city as if a person was very poor, but also how to survive in the middle of the wilderness. Of course not everyone lives in Alaska. Not everyone lives in Hawaii. But everyone lives somewhere near some wilderness. Knowing what to do in cases of survival, will help a person not to be afraid if government fails. What about sharing the survival skills with people in war-torn or religious persecution countries! Our world is still plagued by wars and famines, so knowing wild foods that are edible and how to make bread out of grass seed (one cup of flour can go far), can really help people to overcome fears of our natural world. Knowing how to make a cast out of cat-tail and sticks can help injured people overcome problems when casting isn't available. A class could be entitled, "Surviving the Storms in the Book of Mathew."

Survival skills should almost be an essential in any and all Christians lives, especially if they are serious bible students.

Finally, sustainability is a good way to live life. Do not assume that your local grocery store will always be available. Such thinking is not truth. Small towns lose their economic value, if people do not buy locally. So knowing how to sustain life on your own property or by renting land can help you in the long run. You do not always need to have acre upon acre of land in which a donkey tills that land, but you should know how to sustainably bake your own bread, fill up your pantry with nutrition foods over the winter, how to wash clothes with a wringer and how to keep a supply of herbal concoctions on hand. Knowing how to raise chickens from one generation to another while raising them for local markets can help you economically as well. Keep knowledge found in the books about how people sustained life before the invention of the vehicle on hand. These books will still be valuable in the future as well. A fun class may even be entitled "Book of Romans, the Sustainable Life of Romans and Laura Ingalls Wilder"

13. Etiquette anyone?

Our world is crumbling with lack of respect. Good character is seen as distasteful in this world. God emphasized the need to seek wisdom, to clean up our life and behave more appropriately with our fellow man. A class that includes proper behavior would be a very beneficial class. The class could be entitled "Ladies and Gentlemen and the book of Acts." Include the old books on how ladies should behave and how men should behave as decent citizens of society. Perhaps read books written by Emily Post. Yes, sometimes etiquette ends up on the back burner when families struggle with health issues, financial issues or other negative aspects of life. However, knowing the proper way to act even in difficult situations could possibly restore the person and family back to normal and natural order.

Furthermore, having good etiquette can also aid a person in reaching the lost with the gospel! Being friends with an unsaved person could lead them to church next Sabbath or Sunday or could draw them to a website that promotes bible teachings! Our homes benefit when we have good character and etiquette. In fact, etiquette should be on the top priorities for classes to take. It can show us how to properly share gospel in such a way that we don't become the next "bible thumpers hate xyz" crowd in the news. Etiquette can show the lost how to properly speak to elderly and disabled people. The Psalms and Proverbs are loaded with examples of how we should approach various people with kindness rather than with rejection and reproach. The better etiquette we have, the better tools we will have to overcome the world with the gospel. Many children are in need of good etiquette and respect teachers.

Assignment:

1. Develop a list of art and science classes that you would like to take.
List challenging books you would like to incorporate into each selection.
If you need to, contact a professor at a local college to get some ideas.
Next, create the classes into bible book major classes. Create all the
classes to be focused on both the art or science as well as the bible
book. For example: "Pottery in Africa" will become "Pottery in Africa in
Reflection to the Book of Ezekiel"

2. Write mini summaries for a year of classes from assignment 1, that
you would like to take. Select 8 titles and write summaries for each. If
you would like to, create course syllabi for all eight classes.

Quiz:

Evaluate your understanding of what was presented in this selection:

1. How may a person decide what types of science classes to create?

2. In what ways can you improve your understanding and skills in
music?

3. List all the possible categories of classes that can be created for a
general independent liberal-arts student.

4. Why would an independent student focus more on natural health?

5. How does etiquette help improve life for humanity?

Deuteronomy 31:24

And it came to pass, when Moses had made an end of writing the words of this law in a book, until they were finished,

Tests, Quizzes, Paper Topics, Projects

1. How to create a quiz.

Quizzes that are used in a "Liberal Arts Bible College" class will include biblical knowledge and the secular knowledge. Exodus 35:31, "And he hath filled him with the spirit of God, in wisdom, in understanding, and in knowledge, and in all manner of workmanship;" When it is apparent that a man or woman has truly gained knowledge, understanding and skill, then that man or woman can become fully aware and fully human in their potential towards biblical studies, nature studies and skills. Every quiz should include a combination of all. Some may be thought and reflection questions. Some may be verse memorization questions and some may be knowledge of the topic questions. Asking the student to write an outline of the themes discussed in a classical book would be a good choice for developing a quiz. Quizzes should be based off of lectures, study guide work sheets, reflection papers and more. Don't make the quizzes more than 10-50 points so that it takes an entire class period to complete. Rather make sure the quiz can be completed within

15 minutes at the end of class. The independent student can make the quiz without the use of a professor by creating the quiz after he or she has created his or her study guide. That way the student knows the quiz will be challenging enough to complete. Vocabulary, lists, diagrams and so forth are good resources to use for developing quizzes as an independent student.

2. Questions for a mini report.

A mini paper report asks the student to identify, reflect and research information. The mini report is usually about one or two pages in length double spaced. Even as an independent student, the student should title and align mini papers in a way that appears professional and appealing for a professor to read. Feel free to actually print out the reflection paper.

3. A lecture that leads to greater understanding.

How may a student attend a lecture when they are not actually attending a college? Simple. Read the textbooks out loud. If possible read the teachers manual out loud. Read the bible out loud. Read them into a tape player or recorder of some sort! It's that simple. Of course due to the lack of time, reading a text out loud may not be useful. Furthermore, many times professors will add in additional information which is not found in a text or book. Also, professors help the student understand the text book better and question students about their understanding of the text. I give great credit to wonderful professors who care for the students, and want them to master skills and think outside the textbook. Any skill from computer programming to methods of tree identification or speaking a language are good skills to have.

Instead of attending a "lecture," the independent student should set aside a block of time to create a lecture and questions. Set aside one hour to create diagrams, lists, questions and possible topics a professor may actually discuss. Consider the type of speech and lecture style that a possible professor would use to convey his or her message. Job 41:3 states, "Will he make many supplications unto thee? will he speak soft words unto thee?" As the bible says the teachings and speaking would be soft words, which bring understanding. Also during this time, create study guides which help students study material better. Any method that allows a student to absorb materials presented. Do not be frustrated if you as an independent student simply do not understand quadratic formulas. Work with problems in the answer keys in the back of text books or with on-line materials that help students understand the text better.

If a person is attending an online college or free internet session, lectures will be through video process, so that answers that question of what to do when there is no professor available to give a lecture.

Additional study time will occur outside of lecture time, where study questions are not created and videos or other supplemental materials are not used.

4. Projects large and small

Mini-projects help students learn materials better. Exodus 18:26, "And they judged the people at all seasons: the hard causes they brought unto Moses, but every small matter they judged themselves." In life, there will be big issues we have to face and small issues as well. Without mini-projects, a student may not grasp material presented. Doing things over and over are ways to ensure understanding. Perhaps a project may be to create a poster of the materials presented. Perhaps the project may be to actually go and interview people on the street. Perhaps the project may be to work at a homeless shelter. Perhaps the project may be learning ways to witness to unsaved people. It will all depend on the topic discussed.

Furthermore, good understanding from books and other materials presented may require a few different methods to recall information. For purposes of understanding what is presented, the bible is used as a guide to build understanding, while other texts may also be used in the same manner to build understanding. Four years of college will present these methods of learning as favorable from any age. The following are methods to build greater knowledge: 1. Narrate a passage from the [text/bible] in own words. 2. Draw stick figures of the passages and verses. 3. Skill mentioned In the [text/bible] ? Splinter into small parts and master the skill. 4. Skill mentioned in the [text/bible]? Conquer in short spurts Task-Chore-Task-Chore (variety in month etc). 5. Skill mentioned in the [text/bible]? Specific task same time over and over. 6. Schedule active vs. passive activity. Sing [text/bible] verse, do something else. Write [text/bible] verse, exercise etc. 7. Teach/Learn during high times - 8 P.M. or after a meal etc. Incorporate one verse or passage. 8. Memory moments. In line, while waiting for appointment. Incorporate what you are memorizing with bible verse. 9. Teach for whole body instruction. In [text/bible] passage ID sight, hear, smell etc. 10. Use analogy of object when possible. ie. Use two boards glued together to represent two become one flesh. 11. Drive into inner speech. Say whisper, think random 10 [word, verse, passage]. 12. Sink an emotional hook. ie. Read about 10 plagues then study nature of frogs from [5] sources and give quiz. 13. Get another angle from [word, verse, passage] using any technique listed above. 14. Use placemat grounding. (Timeline, World map, Big lists) Use [text/bible] verse, word passage to id. 15. Train keen details. Use [word, verse, passage] and (draw details, parts, definitions etc) 16. Don't delegate too soon. Do patience/joy 25 x's correctly. ID other positive character words in the bible and do correct with different activities. 17. Practice critical thinking skills with various hot topic mentioned in the [text/bible]. 18. Busy children are happy children. Schedule 10 bible based activities for young children. 19. Teach mastery not just plow through. ID. a bible verse, activity etc. and master it.

Write the above methods down on a note card and laminate it. Instruct yourself to complete any of the learning methods when covering materials. Also consider learning and reading about the methods that regular college students seek to learn more and dig deeper into doing a good job in college study.

5. Testing

Create tests that cover multiple areas. The test should fit into an entire class time hour. Make sure that the tests are more advanced in knowledge and skill than the quizzes and mini-papers. Tests should cover more details than a basic lecture. The tests should cover inner details within books that are essential to know. Even though the independent student "knows" that his test is made of multiple choice answers, he may not remember what answers are the correct answers. Fill in the blank, list things in order, other lists identifications can help test the independent student's knowledge. Asking the student to describe something also helps to test the student's knowledge. By having the student write out or spell out entire verses and phrases from memory, the student can be tested on his knowledge ability more easily. Of course, don't create tests that will confuse or be so far apart from lecture notes, study guides and so forth. Create an outline review paper of test topics about a week before the exam.

Perhaps if one is desiring to develop better test questions, do some research for a book about how professors actually teach students. The book should outline ways to develop good quality testing questions. Do not be afraid to combine ideas from the bible and secular knowledge. Include questions from a resource for a textbook. Maybe there is supplemental material for a text. Include those questions in a test. For example, a test question could go something like this: In the book 2 Chronicles and in chapter 26, we find the illustration of a sixteen year old who become's king. Does this reality seem to work with the teenage population today? Explain why or why not by describing the xyz social dilemmas of teenagers in America. What was the result of this teenage king? Does xyz pattern fit into the social patterns of typical teenage delinquents vs. teenage success who later grow up? Such a question could be asked in a class titled, "2 Chronicles and the American Social Dilemma."

It is good to test student knowledge about once a month along with the quiz knowledge about once a week. It is ok to have a test and a quiz in the same week. To check the quality of the student's ability to complete a test, a set of guidelines and correct answers would be created. An outline of some sort illustrating what answers should be found in thought based test questions.

6. Final Papers

Final papers in a class should cover all the essential elements of research that are necessary to master the skill and to master knowledge of the scripture. In the scripture, we are pointed to the reality that having a pen in hand and writing our ideas on paper is not a bad thing to do. Psalm 45:1, "To the chief Musician upon Shoshannim, for the sons of Korah, Maschil, A Song of loves. My heart is inditing a good matter: I speak of the things which I have made touching the king: my tongue is the pen of a ready writer." Enjoying the communication ability is a process that will develop into a wise student and perhaps later give teaching skills to other students. Perhaps in a music class, the final paper will be the ability of the student to compose music. Perhaps in a biology class the student will complete a lab which identifies various trees as well as various elements in the bible that reflect the nature of trees. Like testing, final papers should have an outline of things that need to be covered in order to get points. The independent student would create a one page paper that would cover the topics which need to be discussed. The student will have an outline which reveals which topics happen to be and what the correct form of answer should appear in a final paper in order for proper grading to take place. Of course, in the process of research an independent student will not "know" the correct answer, but he or she will be able to understand that those topics should be discussed.

Assignment:

1. Create a quiz for a class in economics and the book of Proverbs. Add in vocabulary, bible verses to memorize and fill in the blank. Add any other elements of quizzing that are common for the college student.

2. Create a list of possible paper topics in all the different types of classes. Create possible paper topics that show understanding in both the natural sciences, art and bible. Create enough paper topics to complete all the different subjects of study in a typical liberal arts college. Create enough paper topics to cover major elements of the different types of books in the bible.

Quiz:

Evaluate your understanding of what was presented in this selection:

1. List various elements that should be found within the quiz.

2. In what ways can an independent student rely on a lecture when there is not a professor to guide through the material?

3. List the various methods that can be used to recall information.

4. In what ways can knowledge from bible and knowledge from natural studies be presented in a test?

5. In what types of classes would a lab be used to test understanding?

Job 36:4

For truly my words shall not be false: he that is perfect in knowledge is with thee.

Incorporating Free or Other Internet Classes

1. Make the decision before the year begins.

Before you begin your studies, decide if you want to use internet or free classes. The classes may or may not include video, text book or other resources. When you find a good class, either secular based classes or biblical based classes, determine how you will divide the classes into time slot selections. The use of an internet based class can eliminate a lot of unnecessary wrath, struggle and hassle. Job 5:2 states, "For wrath killeth the foolish man, and envy slayeth the silly one." Being silly and purposefully foolish has led some men to engage in wrath, even Christian men and women. The internet serves as a tool to overcome this. Some good bible study classes can be found through evangelism resources. Perhaps a biblical based resource is through a radio ministry can be helpful. Excellent and challenging college classes can be found through many different colleges. If you would like to learn a basic skill, which includes practice of the skill, like bread making, make sure to decide how many videos from the internet you will include in your classes and how much time you would like to dedicate to internet resource before the year begins.

2. Ensure that you also include aspects relating to biblical major

If you find a good college, that offers challenging courses, make sure that your "bible major" is incorporated into the classes. Ask extra questions about King Hezekiah, if you happen to take a history class online. Create quizzes that include the questions asked from the class as well as extra questions you would like to create based on college major and biblical studies. If you are studying through a bible based class on-line, be sure to include other secular materials if you would like to include that information. Overall, the classes should feel challenging to the student.

3. A separate grade based on independent studies.

Offering a separate grade for the class itself and the actual combination of biblical and secular studies can help the student recognize if he or she is actually applying biblical studies to a secular topic. The independent student can determine his weakness if he can sense where he needs to improve in either secular or biblical studies. Even studies through an internet class, where the questions are already created for the student, can help the student recognize his or her need to improve studies in certain areas. If the class is too difficult, like any college student, the class may need to be dropped. Usually biblical studies classes on the internet are pretty basic and can be followed through with a general education.

Assignment:

1. Find different places that offer internet college level classes. Look for Natural Science, Art and Biblical based classes. Write these down and keep them in mind.

2. Create a schedule for incorporating bible studies into a Natural Science based internet class. Create an additional quiz that would incorporate understanding of the bible along with the studies required.

Quiz:

Evaluate your understanding of what was presented in this selection:

1. Do you need to use internet classes to obtain a liberal arts bible college degree?

2. What makes men fill up with wrath and how do internet classes help overcome this issue?

3. Why should you include biblical studies along with the internet class?

4. Should a independent college student purposefully take easy internet classes?

5. What should a student do if the class is too difficult?

Luke 15:6

And when he cometh home, he calleth together his friends and neighbours, saying unto them, Rejoice with me; for I have found my sheep which was lost.

The Addition of Domestic, Self-Sustainable and Home-Life Classes

1. Enjoyable and effective domestic engineering

Both men and women will need to work in the domestic environment. The home is a person's place of privacy. Without privacy, there may be persecution or forced labor of some sort. Men can know how to work in the kitchen effectively and women can learn how to enjoy washing dishes by hand. Both men and women will have to take out the garbage. The domestic life is for all people. Women who do not enjoy the home but seek to out-do men in some way, may have their priorities mixed up in some way. Such women are not considering the value of making their home pleasant. The home is tranquility. In the bible it speaks that the people of Israel lost their pleasant homes because they forsook the LORD. Ezekiel 26:12 states, "And they shall make a spoil of thy riches, and make a prey of thy merchandise: and they shall break down thy walls, and destroy thy pleasant houses: and they shall lay thy stones and thy timber and thy dust in the midst of the water." Losing a home is not a good experience for anyone, whether it is a mobile home lost due to flood or it is a well established home lost due to war or famine. Men and women approve of living in a pleasant home and want peaceful people to dwell within its walls.

Effective classical housekeeping books are useful knowledge for both men and women. For men such books will simply inform the person about ways people in older times managed deep cleaning in unusual ways and other historical properties, but these things may still be applied even in modern era. Like all secular studies, be sure to include biblical studies as well. Perhaps a class could be entitled "Exodus and the Heart of the Home." Such a class would include ways to study the attitude and how it affects the home. How did the Israelites behave and God's reaction, as well as ways in which to manage a home. Both classic and modern housekeeping books may be studied. Other religious beliefs outside of Christianity may also be studied. Perhaps Judaism homes are different than Buddhism homes in some way. Study these things.

Instead of paying lots of money for a college degree, buy some land and build your own home. Start simple and make it like a cabin. Then when more income is established build bigger and better projects.

2. The fixings of car and home

Men and women will have to do repairs at some point in their life. If a woman doesn't know how to change a light bulb, her life will be very difficult. Of course if that light bulb happens to be inside of a vehicle or other difficult to understand and reach area, this may not be a necessary repair. Both on the grid and off the grid lifestyle should be included in home and vehicle repair. Learn how to light a lantern and make it glow instead of household electric lights for an evening. Ideally, it would be wonderful to learn how to hitch up a few horses, but this may not always be possible for all students. If there is an opportunity to learn how to work with off the grid vehicles and transportation. Definitely take the time to consider it.

Plumbing and safety concerns are issues that people will face. Some people have even studied how chlorine negatively affects human function. Ezekiel 28:4 states, "With thy wisdom and with thine understanding thou hast gotten thee riches, and hast gotten gold and silver into thy treasures." Continuing to know how things function, how things fail, how things are sold to us manipulatively, in our homes, gives us good homes to live within. Perhaps studies on natural well water should be included. What about modernized off-the-grid ways of life? Anything from solar power to wind power. Knowing how these things function can help a person repair these things in his or her own home. Anyone who would like to design their own type of energy should also study these things well before establishing a home if at all possible.

There are many types of homes. Some choose to live in campers long term. Some choose to live in canvas tents and tipi's long term traveling from place to place. Some choose to build their own log-cabin or cob home. Some choose to build a large shed or steel structure for a home, while avoiding unnecessary windows and other such items. Investigate various types of homes that aide people in living a more comfortable life. In fact, those who choose to avoid debt by building their own home are very wise.

3. Cattail mall surprise for enjoyable self sustainability

If you live near cat-tail, you can use this plant for many things. The Native Americans used cat-tail for many things. Learn how to make cordage by rolling the cat-tail, then you will have a free supply of rope and string on hand. Cat-tail can be used to make mats, baskets, ropes, mulch, roof and wall coverings, stuffing (matured heads), and toys (dolls, mini items etc). Cat-tail may also be used as food when young and not tough. Use dyes and other methods to change color of the cat-tail to make a more appealing craft.

4. Frugal Recycling projects

Learning how to melt plastic bags to make other useful items could change your life. Instead of seeing McDonald's cups as throw away items, they could become pottery or places to plant transplants for next year. What about tin-cans. Use a cutting tool and make items for decoration or basic uses around the home. Mat 6:19 says, "Lay not up for yourselves treasures upon earth, where moth and rust doth corrupt, and where thieves break through and steal." Gain more wisdom on how to renew the old. Include a little class that teaches you about frugality and management of time. The days are evil, so make the most of time in a frugal way.

5. Marriage and Family

Should you include marriage and family classes in your studies? Yes. Should you focus only on conservative teachings, or should you focus on liberal teachings as well. It is up to you and how you would like to evaluate and study the family life books. Definitely include study of the biblical families that are illustrated in the bible. 2 Sa 13:32 states, "And Jonadab, the son of Shimeah David's brother, answered and said, Let not my lord suppose that they have slain all the young men the king's sons; for Amnon only is dead: for by the appointment of Absalom this hath been determined from the day that he forced his sister Tamar." This was a sad situation that happened in their home. Study of the life of David and his sons reveals much about the importance of character in the home. Study the positive effects of women's rights, but also study the negative effects of feminism. Feminism being the belief that all men have evil intensions for women most times and that men cannot be centered on love for God and fellow man. Woman's rights being that it is wrong for men to take a young under-developed girl as a bride and it is wrong to take a woman as wife, cause her to have children and then neglect her with paying bills, while the man decides to commit acts of infidelity.

Assignment:

1. Do a search for classical domestic engineering books. List these books and keep them in mind as part of curriculum plan.

2. Find resources that you like that teach you how to create things out of nature and recycled items.

Quiz:

Evaluate your understanding of what was presented in this selection:

1. What causes the people to lose their pleasant homes in Ezekiel? How has the woman's work-force in a fast paced world caused this same effect?

2. What types of things should be studied in order to improve your future home?

3. What types of things may a person make out of cat-tail?

4. What does Jesus say about treasures here on earth?

5. What person's family in the bible can be studied to enhance marriage and family studies?

Esther 1:22

For he sent letters into all the king's provinces, into every province according to the writing thereof, and to every people after their language, that every man should bear rule in his own house, and that it should be published according to the language of every people.

Travel Abroad and Safety with Foreign Groups

1. Is it necessary to travel abroad?

No, it is not necessary to travel abroad to learn more about the world and the way it works. The bible says, Mar 8:36 illustrates, " For what shall it profit a man, if he shall gain the whole world, and lose his own soul?" Usually with internet connection and the ability to read books, you will do fine connecting to people around the world by being open to conversation with them. There are good and bad people in this world, so always consider safety, whatever you may do. If you do happen to travel abroad to a country that does not speak your native language, you may need to take a special class before you go or once you arrive if you are not fluent enough to complete a class of some sort. You may enroll in a community college offered in a specific country. You may also choose to be a volunteer at a hospital, orphanage or other place where people are in need. You can check out the possibility that a host family will allow you to stay in their home for a number of weeks, rather than renting a space or living in a hotel. You may choose to be a missionary by handing out simple bible tracts and bibles, or you may choose not to do that. It is up to you and what you feel you can handle.

2. Using a group travel service

Travel groups may or may not be expensive. When traveling with a group, you may even travel with a gospel sharing group. Mar 16:15 affirms gospel sharing is essential, "And he said unto them, Go ye into all the world, and preach the gospel to every creature." Even if that group is not gospel based, it is still good to keep godly morality in mind, as some in a travel group may not believe the gospel. It can depend on how extensive you would like to do your travels and how risky the travel happens to be. A simple travel group that travels across country to visit outdoor hot spots, like the Rocky Mountains, Utah's arches, Mt. Rushmore or other places in the continental USA would probably not be an expensive travel group. A travel group that visits Europe, Asia, Middle East or Africa would have more expensive needs. While traveling with the group you could turn it into a mini-class, if the travel will take a week or less, or you could turn it into a full class if the travel takes at least one-month time to complete. One could call a class based on actual study of biblical lands, or one could call a class based on interaction with the location and the people during the travels. "Study of Micah in Reflection of Washington D.C. Historical Morality," or "Lands and Places in the Book of Matthew" are a couple of ideas for a class title.

Assignment:

1. List various ministries abroad that you would be interested in working with and for. Perhaps you may not travel to these ministries but you would be willing to give some financial support.

2. List various places close to your home which may be visited and may be traveled to within one day travel time.

Quiz:

Evaluate your understanding of what was presented in this selection:

1. How may a person learn about the cultures of the world without actually traveling to the various places?

2. How can you turn your travels into a ministry? When traveling with a secular group? When traveling with a missionary group?

3. Why is a travel group more expensive?

Romans 15:4

For whatsoever things were written aforetime were written for our learning, that we through patience and comfort of the scriptures might have hope.

Paying for an Actual College Class

1. Inexpensive approach

Community Colleges are generally less expensive than Liberal Arts, Private or Public Universities with the Liberal Arts being the most expensive. Community colleges offer simple skills class that are fairly inexpensive with no need for a student loan, and lead a person to gain better skills in some field whether it's in the arts, literature or electrical off-the-grid lifestyles. Community colleges also offer many skills with animals. Nehemiah 7:68 illustrates, "Their horses, seven hundred thirty and six: their mules, two hundred forty and five." Imagine working properly with that many animals in one setting as written in Nehemiah. Some professions do require safety classes. These may be paid for by an employer, other times they are just good to know types of classes. Look for other places that offer classes. Maybe a certain grocery store is offering cooking classes. Maybe a local nature observatory is offering classes about bird watching. Maybe there is a sport and recreation group that is offering classes in canoeing. Taking up these opportunities to learn from these classes can add knowledge and skill. Like other classes, be sure to incorporate a biblical based study along with the class.

2. Commuter open enroll

If you happen to live near a college which offers four-year degree or higher, you may see if they offer commuter classes. Many Liberal Arts or private colleges prefer their students to live on campus and take at least a certain number of credits to remain enrolled. However, they may also offer community classes, on-line classes or other options for those who are not enrolled full or part-time. Classes from a four-year school or higher will generally be higher in cost. If you do not have a scholarship, you would be wise to have money for such a class paid for in advance. It would be foolish to take such a class, only use it for information and never use such a class in real-life while still hanging onto the debts that were acquired. Keep your bible open if you take a class from a secular resource. In addition, to taking a class entitled "Pottery in the Reformation," consider adding a little extra touch of bible study to the class. Entitle your own assistant class, "Pottery in the Reformation Transformed by the Gospels." When the class takes quizzes, you add in the additional bible study portions that reflect knowledge of the bible and coordination with the class. Essentially, in your records, you would have obtained credits from accredited resource, but your record book will show you all studied bible in a certain way as well in and during the class.

Assignment:

1. List ten community college classes in your area. Write in a few notes about what types of biblical studies you would add to such a class.

2. Look for commuter classes and on-line classes in your area or within decent travel time. List 10 possible classes you may take

Quiz:

Evaluate your understanding of what was presented in this selection:

1. What types of things could you learn about through a Community College as opposed to Liberal Arts College?

2. What places may offer simple mini classes that teach skills?

3. How may you find on-line classes that are offered through a local college?

Nehemiah 9:31

Nevertheless for thy great mercies' sake thou didst not utterly consume them, nor forsake them; for thou art a gracious and merciful God.

Meeting Goals and Deadlines without Distractions

1. Living in my parents or relatives home

Are you safe in your parents home? Are distractions minimal? The bible says there will be divisions, Luke 12:53 says, "The father shall be divided against the son, and the son against the father; the mother against the daughter, and the daughter against the mother; the mother in law against her daughter in law, and the daughter in law against her mother in law." These things will help you determine if your own home is a good place to study. Is there a moral problem in the home in which you grew up? Maybe the family members you grew up with are determined for you to get a four year degree through an accredited university, but they don't want to admit the colleges have ungodly teachings and are very expensive use of time and energy. Maybe you grew up on a farm and there is a cabin which you may use as a study. Are there other community members around who want to take your time out of your schedule and encourage you to party and live an immoral lifestyle? What about parents who do little to encourage you in secular studies, but only want you to attend to bible studies all the time, not considering the possible negative effects this could have. You are more than capable of making educational, knowledge and wisdom choices if you have attained a full high school or even eighth-grade education! An eighth grade education can help you succeed in work and in life more than most people realize. Most people actually read materials suitable for a 5th to 8th grade level of reading every day of their career. However, you can function on learning many things as well. Knowledge puffs up, but love of home and family lasts forever. It would be a blessing to have family and relatives who are supportive when you are able to attain high grades in high school levels, but wish to study independent studies and take such studies seriously.

2. Out on my own

Maybe you may need to move to a different community if the environment where you live is not safe. Drugs, alcohol, prostitution, gambling, pharmaceutical dependency and so forth, hinder a person's ability to attain good quality studies and good moral value. Mat 19:29 illustrates, "And every one that hath forsaken houses, or brethren, or sisters, or father, or mother, or wife, or children, or lands, for my name's sake, shall receive an hundredfold, and shall inherit everlasting life." Yes, these are problems, but one simply cannot function as a student when others force immorality on you. After you have studied, you may then safely approach and be a missionary of some sort to people of this type who make choices like this, but in the mean time, it is best to move away from these influences. Unfortunately these types of influences are commonly found on college campuses. This is why study of the bible alone is unpopular on secular campuses. Furthermore, even Christian campuses which boast of allowing people of Christian faith inside their dorms, simply cannot always obtain strict rules on their students to eliminate those of poor character. Sexual promiscuity can be found inside the doors of Christian Campuses because children of strict parents depart from their Christian upbringing, believing that such biblical values were a lie to begin with. Such a terrible fault of those who hate bible studies, but yet claim Christian teachings as their own. Sadly even seminaries can boast of sexual impurity, down to the very core as being the ultimate design for humanity. Oh, Christ please stir up the hearts of people to love you more and self, less!

A good starting place to begin being on one's own may be in house sharing with an elderly person. Their lack of financial income and companionship, may allow you to settle in their space. However, be aware that an elderly person who does not respect privacy will not be a good home for a student to obtain, complete and succeed in studies. Social dilemmas present themselves from time to time with elderly persons, even if they mean well.

What about camping? Long term camping is possible from late winter up until the late fall, depending on the zone where one lives. Or what about building one's own cabin in the woods. If one takes the time to study at the local library, the extra hours outside of work can be spent building a simple cabin in the woods. Purchase a little bit of land, carry in water jugs and toiletry. One who knows how to function in simple carpentry, will have a better chance at not fearing the words of men of disdain. Also, consider churches that have kindness and compassion towards biblical ideals. God may offer blessing through a home available for guests.

3. Continuing with my home church and community activity

The blessing of being an independent student is that you do not have to move away from the community that you love! The bible says blessing comes to those who serve others. Mat 20:27 declares, " And whosoever will be chief among you, let him be your servant." You can continue attending the community events that are good in your area. You do not have to ignore elderly widows whom you have enjoyed visiting. You do not have to stop participating as a volunteer for a local library's children's picnic. You may safely participate in these things while obtaining a major in the book of the bible via. independent liberal art bible college degree. In fact, you will feel more connected to the concerns of your local community and connected to the people if you do not have to transfer to a different community from the one in which you grew up. However, there are political people who beg you to enhance your talents through a college. These people are not concerned for you. These people are political people not interested in visiting the disabled, the orphans and the widows in the community. Do not be hindered by these people who are more interested in selfish degree attainment, rather than diligent study of God's word.

Assignment:

1. Think of people and events in your community or area that are positive influence for individual heartfelt needs and for the local community needs. Write 20 things down. Choose to participate in a few of these things this year.

2. List a few people in your area whom have pressured you to obtain higher degrees, especially pay large sums of money for those degrees. Pray for them.

Quiz:

Evaluate your understanding of what was presented in this selection:

1. List problems in some homes that could create havoc in a bible college or liberal arts degree students life.

2. Why are college campuses sometimes viewed as good places to live due to less violence in general, but are in-fact filled with immoral living and support of it?

3. How late may a person camp if they choose to live at a camp-ground?

4. List the different types of people in your community that would enjoy having you visit. List different types of events in your local community that are positive.

5. True/False Christian college campuses are always supportive of biblical morality and always safe.

Proverbs 21:5

The thoughts of the diligent tend only to plenteousness; but of every one that is hasty only to want.

Working while Completing Studies

1. Skill based work

One can plant an orchard, to obtain skills related to caring for trees. Income will not be possible from such an orchard until the trees have grown for at least ten years. A person can plant a large garden. The produce from the garden may be sold in a little bit at a time or in large bulk. The garden produce can be variety with many skills in how to work with different types of plants, or it can be three or four varieties. People in biblical times also enjoyed the labor of gardening. Son 6:11 pronounces, " I went down into the garden of nuts to see the fruits of the valley, and to see whether the vine flourished, and the pomegranates budded." A small storage shed may be purchased or rented. Within that storage shed a person may buy and sell items. Anything may be sold on eBay or other internet resources. Perhaps crafts can be created and stored in the storage shed. Working with lumber? Maybe simple boxes can be created and stored in the storage shed to sell by internet or at a local store. The skills obtained will be beneficial. Volunteer work will also help a person to obtain more workable skills. The goal with skill based work, is not necessarily income, but enjoyment of work and obtaining of skills.

2. Income based work

Some work could be income based. As a woman, there is a possibility that you will need to work from home or be a homemaker at some time in order for the home to function. It simply is not possible for a woman to work out side of the home or in the home when she has young children, unless she is seriously not into Christian beliefs and truly believes in daycare system. Mar 3:29 illustrates, "But he that shall blaspheme against the Holy Ghost hath never forgiveness, but is in danger of eternal damnation." There are other times where a husband is ill, or morally unstable, and the wife needs to work. Perhaps the income based work could be self-employment types of work. Anything from housecleaning, to gutter clearing. Perhaps some of the work may be through an agency such as babysitting agency. Never choose income based work that Is contrary to biblical ideals. That could mean turning down the job as a wedding dress model, simply because the pictures require a woman to hold a bottle of champagne. Stumbling block incomes are not good if one chooses biblical based living. It could also mean in some cases to turn down the job as an office assistant at a hospital if it turns out that the hospital regularly aborts unborn children. What about working at a casino? Although the income may be possible, would it necessarily be a good job for a Christian to obtain? It will all depend on the situation.

Assignment:

1. Look into finding information about a storage shed to store things to sell. Start selling things in various ways. On-line, in person and other ways to sell simple items.

2. Look at local job listings. Circle all the jobs that may have potential to be more godly in nature such as working at a hardware store.

Quiz:

Evaluate your understanding of what was presented in this selection:

1. How many years will it take for an orchard to be available for income generation?

2. What type of skills are obtained through volunteer work?

3. What types of careers would not be good choices for Christian participation unless under persecution?

Job 20:3

I have heard the check of my reproach, and the spirit of my understanding causeth me to answer.

How to Check for Effective Learning and Spiritual Growth

1. Consult professionals in the field

How may an independent student check to see if his knowledge is effective and his reasoning is clear? He may work with current professionals in the field. He may visit an actual farm and test to see if he knows enough about various farming practices on that farm. As the verse says, some types of work are not exciting, but are taxing on a person's time, energy and desires. Exodus 5:9 states, "Let there more work be laid upon the men, that they may labour therein; and let them not regard vain words." Perhaps he wishes to study "Farm Ownership." In that case, consult the farmer and ask how he manages to keep up with farm ownership of land. He may directly ask to help with taxes or other things of that nature. He may help with unloading apples, and reporting on the accounts and balances for selling those apples. Furthermore, one may check physicians' desk references and acquire skills in CNA training to understand more about the healthcare field without going further into pharmaceutical style medical degrees. Instead, choose naturopathic or herbalist fields of study. What about antiques? There again, write up a paper on antiques and see if a local antique dealer would approve the paper as being sufficient in knowledge. Then there is also the pastor, preacher, lawyer and other people who make money for talking. What about midwifery, car-dealers, book writers, news anchors and more. Check out the yellow pages of a phone book. Decide what skills you would like to know more about. Study what they study for a day or two. Ask what books they read. Do what they do. Practice the skills in speaking that they practice. One does not actually have to pay for a college degree to get professional skills. Professionalism is a term for those who regularly work in and with a certain set of principles or with a certain type of people. It does not mean that you cannot attain those same understandings. It just means that you need to practice those skills yourself.

2. Sell some products, books and creations

One way to know if you are succeeding in learning effectively is to sell some products. If a student has created the class, "Recycling Arts and the Book of Ruth," try selling a few hand drawings of Ruth gleaning in the fields. Perhaps do some prints of wheat onto a bread basket, write in some verses from Ruth. To determine if you are learning your skill well, your ability to sell your product is a sure way to determine if you are successful in the skill. Mini-eBooks are a simple way to express what you have learned. Write about what you learned in a "Teaching Children Under 7 by the Book of Ezekiel" class. Write such a book in an e-book format. Do not be afraid if you do not feel that your writing is worthy of much attention. Simply make sure your grammar is reasonable for people to understand what you are trying to communicate. Fill up your book and your work with God's word. Deuteronomy 6:9 says, "And thou shalt write them upon the posts of thy house, and on thy gates." Be very aware that many people make income in bad ways. They believe they are good people for making such income but they are actually a stumbling block for weak people. Perhaps their income is alcohol based income or frivolous sexuality products based income. Do not let these negative people deter you or influence you towards income in that way. Even a nice grocery store could carry many good items, but some bad items are within. However, some good items that are sold, could be used in bad ways by bad people, so we can't always make full judgment when it comes to selling products.

When your creations are positive, they are pleasing to use in your own home. Various creations may also be used in your home and in your environment. Perhaps you are determining ways to re-use sun-flower stalks, so you preserve the sun-flower stalks for a later use in your garden or yard. Doing these things will help you grow in your knowledge and skill and will also help you determine if you have learned both secular knowledge and spiritual-biblical knowledge.

3. Letter of support from a professor

Perhaps when a person is going to develop a class, it is a good idea to write to an actual professor. The bible itself encourages people to take note of happenings. The word of God encourages good language and communication skills! Isa 30:8 says, "Now go, write it before them in a table, and note it in a book, that it may be for the time to come forever and ever:"   You could inform the professor that you are an "independent student." You may or may not inform the professor that you are interested in biblical studies as well. It would depend on the type of professor that you are writing. You may or may not inform the professor the title of your class. Simply state that your focus will be in anthropology or in astronomy. Informing a professor about the books you will be reading and using as textbook, the topics you will look into as well as other important aspects will help the professor to understand how to give you advice when developing your class. The more support and encouragement you receive, the more success you will have when doing your studies. The professor may also suggest additional books to study along with the ones you plan to use in your class.

4. Feelings of strength rather than feelings of defeat

If you have a feeling that you are not succeeding in physics study, you may need to consult a tutor! Yes, tutors can help you as an "independent student" just like any other student. You may find them at a local college or you may find them on-line. Asking questions helps you succeed. The bible informs us that we should be aware of intelligent people as gifts. Deuteronomy 1:13 says, "Take you wise men, and understanding, and known among your tribes, and I will make them rulers over you."   The gifts of a wise man should be used for others and not for selfish reasons and uptight pride filled nonsense. Typically the tutor received a B+ or greater grade in the class or the tutor passed a certain test, hence he was qualified to be a tutor in that area of study. Do not be afraid to ask an actual artist in basketry for assistance if you cannot seem to create a basket out of cat-tail, but you would like to do that perfectly. What about bible study? Do you feel burdens lifted by adding in bible studies to your classes? Do you feel the studies have become too hard since bible studies have been added? Have you been able to write articles about psychology topics in relationship study of scripture alongside secular studies. Do you sense the strength of wisdom that comes from the scripture over the strength of man-made laws, rules and regulations? If you can, then you are succeeding in understanding both biblical and secular topics. If you are able to complete entire biblical studies each day without distraction, then your habit of bible study is being established. If you are able to absorb biblical topics as you read them, then you are also absorbing what you need from scripture.

Assignment:

1. List various professionals in your area, or abroad that you would consider consulting for information.

2. Start up an internet based income generation. Make things look professional. Be sure to sell at road-side stands and markets as well.

Quiz:

Evaluate your understanding of what was presented in this selection:

1. How may a student study with a farmer?

2. What ways can the internet be used to make income? What ways should it not be used to make income?

3. What types of negative influence things do people sell that Christian should avoid selling as a private vendor?

4. What verse indicates that God wants people to use good language and communication skills?

5. Does God give credit to wise men?

Matthew 7:15

Beware of false prophets, which come to you in sheep's clothing, but inwardly they are ravening wolves.

Internet Preachers, Televangelist, Radio Hosts and Spiritual Books

1. Are these actually effective teaching tools?

These may or may not be effective teaching tools. Yes, one should look up the negative warning signs about the spiritual lives and conditions of a televangelist before opting to use his or her resources. Some are very flashy and pride filled televangelists who use a lot of biblical talk, but no real down-to-earth overcoming of internal sin. As the bible verse says, those who suffer for him are reigning with him. 2Ti 2:12 clearly states, " If we suffer, we shall also reign with him: if we deny him, he also will deny us." Some televangelists actually do take the time to look directly into the bible and ask people to do so as well. Can their teachings be applied? Yes, generally these teachings can be applied especially if they consider that there is human suffering in this world and it is because of lies and deceptions that attempt to control and distort realities of what it means to have a change in heart. Be aware, that using a popular teaching from a man or woman who is caught in lies, fornication or other serious sin, will not be useful for you or for anyone as far as biblical knowledge is concerned. A man or woman who once sought to overcome problems in abortion or marriage failures, may have some good "ideas" as his teachings are based on biblical truth, but he becomes hypocritical in his ordeals, then one should only consider such teachings if that man is over the age of 40 and has more roots in his life to overcome the burdens of raising home and family. A man in grandpa stage who has shown that he can lead his own sons and daughters to the biblical truths of home, marriage and family will be a better option for resource than a man who praised large families but failed to acknowledge the aspects of freedom that come from scripture alone to overcome internal evils. Men in their youth may know there is a right and wrong, but fail to understand the fruits until they are older and have true biblical knowledge, meditation in their life.

On the other hand, there may be some good radio show hosts who are not as well known. These should definitely be considered a more reliable resource. Commentary from men who diligently study scripture has been shown to have lasting impact on human lives even after such men die. Consider using these as resource for biblical study as their moral fruits have come to fruition. False attacks against these godly men overcame by the power of the word in their lives. Even a female who considers her world-view without bible as good and solid, will be found to be at fault when facing such men of scripture knowledge and meditation.

2. How to discern if the preaching is focused on 'the word'

First, use a concordance or computer to search for specific words. If these things are mentioned in the bible, you can perhaps use their teachings. If the words are not found in the bible and aligning with the verses, the teachings may be geared to false reality. Success as termed in the bible is a reflection of God's law and wanting to follow it, not a reflection of a preacher in some way. Joshua 1:8 says, "This book of the law shall not depart out of thy mouth; but thou shalt meditate therein day and night, that thou mayest observe to do according to all that is written therein: for then thou shalt make thy way prosperous, and then thou shalt have good success." A bible teacher who is teaching on success and shows all the verses that relate to success may be a reliable resource if he points out that men need to do something rather than just giving money to something which is not related to helping the less fortunate. Are the teachings encouraging men to study the bible more? Are the teachings encouraging men to trust a certain type of ministry rather than just the word itself? The more focus there is on scripture itself, on doing something for the Lord rather than for self, the better the reliability of such teachings. The more one focuses only on particular denomination and on not acknowledging internal sins, is a sign that the teachings are not reliable.

3. Possible denominations: Independent Baptist, Anabaptist, Seventh Day Adventist, Messianic, Liberal denominations, Non-Denominational

There are possible denominational choices which offer good teachings on biblical topics. Among those could be Independent Baptist. These teachings encourage people to memorize scripture and get more knowledge of the word itself. Anabaptist encourages a basic Christian life without so much attachment to fixing this world in ungodly ways. Seventh-Day-Adventist is not as popular or known for biblical resource, but the teachings about the bible are essentially the same and sometimes more detailed than one would find in a Baptist type of church. Essentially, one is encouraged to take the bible literally in the Seventh-Day-Adventist denomination without burden of law. Messianic teachings could be more of a Hebraic roots style, or it may be more Orthodox Jewish in nature. Either way, such teachings help a person understand the literal biblical stories actually did occur many years ago. Liberal denominations offer teachings as well. Like all denominations, there are some things that should not be considered as scripture based but as promoting the particular denomination. If the resources are from any of the more liberal denominations from Lutheran to Episcopal or even Catholic, consider if the teaching is reflecting actual biblical truths or not. For example, a teaching about pro-life movements would be appropriate from a liberal church mindset. A teaching about helping the poor would be appropriate from a liberal church mindset. A teaching about how polygyny helps the Mormon Church grow, can be useful for Mormons only. While a teaching about how polygyny was practiced by early Jewish people and even early Christians can be useful information for Christian thought as God desires family to stay together. A teaching about how homosexuality has improved the condition of the church is not appropriate from a liberal church mindset. As the bible says, some will give over to false teachings and unbiblical reasoning in the last days! 1Ti 4:1 says, "Now the Spirit speaketh expressly, that in the latter times some shall depart from the faith, giving heed to seducing spirits, and doctrines of devils;" Such teachings are from below and are not from heavenly origin. Same as the liberal denominations, a non-denominational church may offer biblical teachings. If the teaching is a summary of a bible story in their own words, such a teaching may be considered. If the teaching is an encouragement for more wealth and not following the suffering that Christ suffered, it really would not be worth the time to listen to such teachings.

Over all, the best teacher is Jesus himself. Next would be elders who are godly, know biblical truths, are not false-accusers and not persuaded of false teachings which are not found in bible. After the elders, would be solid biblical scholars who have studied and apply the bible to life.

Assignment:

1. Look up ministries that teach the bible appropriately. Look up ministries that serve as cornerstones to the Christian faith. Search for ministries who are prosperity preaching types of ministries and do not promote bible study but worship of a pastor.

2. Write down classical literature that comes from certain denominations (ie. Luther, Calvin, Augustine, Menno Simons etc). Write down Christian literature that comes from 200 years ago or less (ie. Ellen White, Spurgeon, Martin Luther King Jr. etc). Write down modern day writings that apply to the heart from various denominations in both liberal and conservative view (ie. Joyce Meyer, Ben Carson, Benny Hinn, un-named Mennonite writers etc). Include biblical commentary and children's literature as well. Egermeir and amplified bible stories.

Quiz:

Evaluate your understanding of what was presented in this selection:

1. Can all televangelist be trusted as bible teachers?

2. What are signs that a radio, or television host has good teachings?

3. What indications are there that a ministry is not encouraging the elimination of sin in a person's life?

4. What types of teachings encourage more bible study from a particular denomination?

5. What types of denominations try to avoid bible study, but it would be ok to read the classical literature?

1Timothy 6:8

And having food and raiment let us be therewith content.

Shelter During Two or Four Years of Classes

1. Parents, guardians and close family up until age 20

A young adult who is godly and a family who encourages their child to be godly, is a good shelter resource for the independent student. A young adult who does not want to be social in a positive way, wants to find boyfriend or girlfriend and wants to play video games or think upon negative things should not be allowed in the godly parent's home as they are not living a godly life but a selfish life. 1Co 7:15 says, "But if the unbelieving depart, let him depart. A brother or a sister is not under bondage in such cases: but God hath called us to peace." However, the grown child who has repented of these behaviors and would like to study peacefully, without riotous living may safely stay in the parents' home for study. Some children may simply choose to use a community college to gain further skill. This may be necessary to further ones career. If the young adult lives in the home, the parents would be wise in requesting that the unmarried child not socialize "privately." This is because the lure and temptation to seek advice from ungodly youth and other people is so strong. No private e-mail account and no private mail-box should be established for the young person who is under the age of 20. Godly parents can help prevent fraudulent financial handlings. Credit card debt is a terrible thing for a young person to acquire who has not even started the basic life principles to survive! However, if the family does not want the young-adult to be godly or would like the young-adult to be abused verbally or accept insults, living in parents home may not be the best choice. This may even occur in families where it was believed that the parents were godly in nature, but little elements of sin choice were aloud in the home.

2. Parents, guardians and close family up until age 25 or marriage

As long as you can safely get along with your family up until age 25, you can live with your family. Even though our world is getting faster and faster, the wicked ideas move faster and faster too. So like the student who stays with family until age 20, the independent student who lives with family until marriage or age 25, is wise in doing so. Num 8:24 indicates age by this verse, "This is it that belongeth unto the Levites: from twenty and five years old and upward they shall go in to wait upon the service of the tabernacle of the congregation." However, if one would like to, he or she can begin buying one's own home after studies are completed. Whether it's at the age of 19 or at the age of 21, starting to create one's own home is a good idea. A person does not need to live in that home until marriage or until age 25, however, to save energy bills, hassle of cleaning and harassment from immature young adults. Furthermore, like age 20 adults, it is best to not have private accounts by internet or general postal mail, except for banking accounts, outside of the parental guidance until age 25 or when a man or woman is married. Why? Well, the temptation to believe in independence whether it's in money or in conversation, outside of God's word grows at an alarming rate once a child starts "thinking" and "believing" in self-righteous living. However, if the family an independent student grew up with is not godly, or is shaky in their understanding of scripture, it is best to seek the counsel of friends and church groups who understand the need for godly living and lifestyle particularly in the young adult. Ensure that they can help you eliminate the addiction to fast paced communication life style, until more maturity is established. Maybe a young woman would decide not to pursue getting a driver's license in order to eliminate the desire for excess expense and unnecessary independent living. A wise young woman will buy a plot of land and begin a garden, wIthout the strings of this world attached at her hip. No man or woman should want to attend every seminar, party, or escape route to selfish living if they want to live a more biblical life. Marriage invitations, companionships and so forth that encourage riotous living should be avoided in the independent biblical students life. It is ok and possible to observe the people and the effects of riot living, like the effects that happened to Job, however, just avoid joining them.

During this stage of life, a betrothal may be in the process or a career may be beginning, especially if all studies are completed. Some "independent students" may choose to continue their studies into an early married life. After the difficulty of a four year degree program is completed, studies may continue into more advanced levels as the independent student desires. Perhaps there may even be a higher educational school that is willing to work with a successful independent studies student. If the student demonstrates many abilities in multiple areas of study as well as long lasting credibility towards knowledge in bible or other sources, a further education beyond bachelor level may be attainable. Career plans should also begin in this stage of life if it hasn't already. The typical "independent student" could do anything from working as a small business owner to setting up a crafting studio. Perhaps book writing may be in mind, or working with the disabled in some way. There really is no limit. However, assume that if a more risky career path is decided upon, that a back-up career for financial capability should be established. A resume will simply indicate "independent college student" or a personally derived title, under the title of college on a work application. This may seem confusing, but a general list of the books read, biblical knowledge advanced and skills obtained will be perfect, for the eyes of the curious world.

3. Parents, guardians and family up until age 30

If the family is a godly family in the "independent biblical student's" life, then living with family even up until age 30 may be possible. Perhaps the "independent bible student" went away for two to four years to complete studies but then returns home. If the parents are willing to work with the student, then the student may stay in the parents' home and work with their fellowship as socially acceptable means to successful living. After the age of 25, most young adult temptations will have passed away. The lure and grip for selfish living disappear if no serious companionship with worldly people was ever established. On the other hand, spiritual blindness continues to exist in the adult that is under the age of 30. Luke 3:23 says, "And Jesus himself began to be about thirty years of age, being (as was supposed) the son of Joseph, which was the son of Heli," For men, the spiritual blindness exists until about an age older than for women. If the older adult is not married and is peaceful with parents or extended family, he or she can peacefully work out an agreement for living in the same space. Such living choices can cause the burden of debt in early mortgage payments to disappear. Even in some cases a married couple may live with older family members. Do be wise and careful in such living environments, however. If a man doesn't leave his father and mother, the father and mother of that man may say untrue, hurtful and scornful thing to a new wife. This is not pleasant. Never allow extended family to live under the same roof, unless absolute privacy and separate escape routes are possible to the newlywed couple. Noises from television sets, addiction problems can bother newlywed couples. Even addiction problems in more godly family members can be sensed. So living with extended family in same roof should only be used in emergency situations. It is better to live in a camper in a campground than to share a home with extended family when a couple is married. Harassments will not be as evident in such situations.

4. On my own in an apartment

There is a possibility that you may move into an apartment. You could ask for a room-mate or two to help save costs of living in an apartment. The cost for room and board will go down significantly with the assistance of roommates who will help pay for a place to live. Make sure that each individual tenant pays directly to the land-lord in their own time. Luke 22:12 says, "And he shall shew you a large upper room furnished: there make ready." Perhaps one envelope can have two or three different payees. This would help ensure each person takes their own responsibility. If you are aware that there are moral consequences with some room-mates be sure to include those issues in writing before rooming up with someone else. Typically, a college will give a survey to each new student. This would include likes and dislikes about noise, temperature, social life and so forth. Having such a survey before sharing an apartment is a good idea. Be sure to include that you are not into drinking, smoking and other ungodly behaviors! Beware as well, some roommates may question biblical adequacy. This can be confusing to a person under 20 years old. If the roommate is not a Christian and does not study bible along with you in some way, it may not be wise to share a room with such an individual. Why is this not a good option for a room-mate? Because such a roommate will distract you from the biblical portion of the independent liberal arts bible college study.

5. On my own in a tent, outdoor land or other housing

This is a possibility as well. If one goes camping from early spring until late fall, one will not have to face the hassle of spending a lot of energy and time setting up a special dorm room. Isa 54:2 says, "Enlarge the place of thy tent, and let them stretch forth the curtains of thine habitations: spare not, lengthen thy cords, and strengthen thy stakes." Of course, if a person does choose an outdoor living arrangement, make sure to include the possibility that bad weather may arise. Live in a solid canvas tent, rather than a tent made of cheap fabrics. To save on costs for camping in a campground, for adventure one could try to travel with rendezvous groups as they arrange camping on larger groups. Another possibility is to see if a farmer would let you live on a space of his land for a season or two. Then there is also the possibility of other types of housing. Living in a camper in someone's driveway for a season wouldn't be a bad idea, as long as you have some sort of access to a shower every now and then. Simply put an ad in a newspaper and ask if there is a home that would allow you to park your camper on their driveway, then go to a campground get washed up and other such things. For water and electricity it is up to the home-owner if they would allow you to use theirs for a price, otherwise simply carry in some water jugs.

Assignment:

1. List several qualities that indicate that it is safe to live in your parents or guardians home. List several qualities that it is not safe to live a biblical life in your parents or guardians home. Write a verse next to the qualities.

2. Look at the costs of living in various locations whether it is in a tent, or an apartment or other dwelling.

Quiz:

Evaluate your understanding of what was presented in this selection:

1. List qualities for and against living with parents and guardians up until the age of 20.

2. Why is it good to seek protective social covering from adult-like temptations before the age of 25?

3. At what age does spiritual blindness start to disappear?

4. Should a bible studies student always trust that their Christian roommate is truly Christian?

5. What type of tent would be suitable if a student wants to choose camping as a way to live?

Genesis 41:36

And that food shall be for store to the land against the seven years of famine, which shall be in the land of Egypt; that the land perish not through the famine.

Nutrition and Food Preparation

1. Family style meals

These types of meals offer much warmth in our cold world. A full, family style meal makes home feel like home. A complete meal with meat, vegetable, bread, side-dish and desert takes a lot of time to prepare. Matthew 13:33 says, "Another parable spake he unto them; The kingdom of heaven is like unto leaven, which a woman took, and hid in three measures of meal, till the whole was leavened." Normally in day to day life, one will not have enough time to prepare a family style meal. If it is possible to eat such a meal with a close family, this would be a better option than no meal at all. Because the independent college student is free to study as he or she chooses, there is more possibility for the student to get into study of the skill of meal preparation and formal etiquette in such meals. However, generally as the bible says, a meal of herbs is better than a stalled ox. So in the long run, though it is fun and interesting to eat fancy meals with delicious meats and fancy vegetables, it is far better to have goodness, mercy good character along with a bowl of herbs.

2. Preplanned meals

There is a possibility that you, as an independent student, may preplan your meals. Here is an example of a woman who readily worked at keeping up with cooking. 1Sa 25:18 indicates, "Then Abigail made haste, and took two hundred loaves, and two bottles of wine, and five sheep ready dressed, and five measures of parched corn, and an hundred clusters of raisins, and two hundred cakes of figs, and laid them on asses." Keeping a set of plastic plates on hand can help you develop a set of frozen meals. Having about 30 to 60 plates as well as a deep freezer can help a person create meals for up to a month. Create a list of 12 or more meals that you like and have balance in nutrition. Purchase all that is needed in bulk and large supply. Prepare meats in advance, stir-fry the foods, sauté the vegetables and other methods of food preparation that allow for easy thaw and cooking in order to eat the meal. Cover the plate with wax paper or freezer paper. Tape the cover to the plate with masking tape and label appropriately with directions, contents and date. Not only can a student prepare their own meals, he or she may also purchase store prepared frozen meals as well. A person will not save as much money by using these types of meals, but the possibility to use these meals can help fill in the gaps and make meal time easier to accomplish.

3. Eating out

Eating out is not highly recommended for the independent college student. Once a month is usually plenty, considering the expense and sometimes nutrition habit that goes with eating out. The psalmist illustrates the use of eating out as a special table before the enemies. Psalm 23:5 says, "Thou preparest a table before me in the presence of mine enemies: thou anointest my head with oil; my cup runneth over." Be careful of using convenience store foods as meals. No planning goes into eating convenience foods, so little nutrition is considered and little time is considered when budgeting such meals. Eating out at fast food restaurants, should rarely occur in the young adult, as improper eating habits are established. If the independent college student is concerned that he or she may run out of time for meal preparation from time to time, simply keep some granola bars, fresh fruit in a bowl, peanut butter and crackers on hand at all times. That way there is never an excuse to eat on the run or to eat out for no purpose at all than to avoid meal preparation.

Occasionally it is OK to eat out. Perhaps the independent college student lives near a college campus. It is ok to eat on campus. Some independent college students may even work on such a campus! The college campus has an actual cafeteria, special healthy convenience store and maybe a diner or two. There is also a possibility that the independent student would like to take advantage of the possibility that eating at a fancy restaurant with a friend or companion would be a fine idea. Save up the money and choose to do this on a weekend or during a special occasion.

4. Ensure the best nutrition

Basic nutrition can actually easily come from knowing how to make a bowl of porridge. One doesn't have to bake every loaf of bread ever eaten when doing independent studies, but one can ensure basic nutrition by making simple whole food choices. Even biblical people accepted basic meal and grain as good food. Gen 18:6 says, "And Abraham hastened into the tent unto Sarah, and said, Make ready quickly three measures of fine meal, knead it, and make cakes upon the hearth." A week long menu for an independent student, with no access to a college cafeteria could be something like this: Breakfast - cornflakes, toast, apple, oatmeal, Fruit bar, bagel, Lunch - Cheese or lunchmeat sandwich & Green Beans, Cornmeal mush & honey toast, Lunchmeat sandwich wrap & fresh vegetable salad, Tomato soup & grilled cheese sandwich, Nuggets & Fries, Baked potato & Salsa, Pasta Sauce & Carrots, Supper - Salmon & cheese sandwich & Beets, Pickled Herring & Pickles & crackers, Pizza & bread sticks & Salad, Tuna sandwich & steamed greens & pudding, Vegetable Soup & ramen noodles & Pickled beets, Fried cabbage & cheese sauce & toast, Ramen Noodles & Tuna Sauce & Peas, Multigrain mush & honey & smoothie, Stir-fry & Crackers, hard boiled eggs & Toast etc.

Include fruits and healthy deserts in these menus as well. From the menu, mix and match what works best for your tastes. Include cabbage or kale in your menu if you are choosing recipes that are frugal to ensure high vitamin content. Include oatmeal, cornmeal and other mush types of cereals If you would like a good bulky filling food that is quite frugal in cost. Eggs are cheap and easy to boil for a complete protein for a meal. Vegetarian style diets can be cheaper if done wisely, particularly choices in rice, beans and stir fry. Overall, the college student fridge should be sufficient enough to include vegetables, fruits and simple to prepare frozen choices. Avoid cheap frozen dinners if at all possible, due to the poor quality of the foods. Avoid constantly eating Mac-and-cheese, canned soups and other prepared food meals. These are usually high in sodium, sugars and low in nutrition.

Furthermore, it is best to choose fasting for general health than to choose fad diets to accomplish a certain weight. Fasting has been shown to restore the body into balance that it needs. A fruit fast can save money and keep the body restored. Fasting is much easier to accomplish in college years before children are brought into the home. Some children are not apt to enjoy fasting, so this can be frustrating to an adult. An adult can easily accomplish fasting and safely do so. Other experiments with nutrition and diets that are used to achieve better food goals are best accomplished before the home is established! Perhaps a native American diet is desired with tasting all natural meals with grass seed flour and crow for soup and stew. Or perhaps a special fermentation food diet is desired. Making sourdough bread during the college years is a good habit to establish before the home and family begin.

Assignment:

1. Create a plan for home-made frozen dinners.

2. Learn how to make simple and nutritious foods. Things like oatmeal, cornmeal and fried cabbage.

Quiz:

Evaluate your understanding of what was presented in this selection:

1. True/False An independent college student who is serious in his or her studies will have enough time to prepare family style meals.

2. How many meals should be planned in order to create a month's worth of frozen dinner meals?

3. True/False Independent College students should frequently eat at fast food places because they are convenient and cheap.

4. True/False Independent College students may not eat on a regular college campus.

5. List nutritional foods that are simple, frugal and easy to make.

Esther 8:16

The Jews had light, and gladness, and joy, and honour.

Extracurricular

1. Sport

Taking up sports without enrollment in a college can be lightly difficult, but is not impossible. Positive lifelong sports would include biking, running, hiking and raking some leaves. Heb 12:1 says, "Wherefore seeing we also are compassed about with so great a cloud of witnesses, let us lay aside every weight, and the sin which doth so easily beset us, and let us run with patience the race that is set before us," Developing physical fitness habits by enrolment in a fitness club may help develop more muscle and build some friendships. Sometimes sport clubs allow you to participate in a little sand volley ball game or other activity. Unfortunately, due to the lack of spiritual growth in people's lives, people are not connected to each other appropriately, so sport can become spiritual drain on human life. Simple sport activity is fine, but beware that this replaces spiritual values. It does not. Lonely feelings and rejection feelings simply occur because a person has not found Christ as savior and redeemer. As a result, any sporting activity in college may not exist after college graduation because most of the population is not involved in every sporting activity. Overall, sport is fun and enjoyable, especially if one decides to go rock climbing or scuba diving, but it is most enjoyable if Christ and spiritual value are considered along with the sport. All in all, some folks may decide to actually enroll in a college so that he or she can teach sport classes. This may be fine, but like all things, consider the costs that go along with enrolling in actual colleges vs. simply doing the study as an independent or part-time student.

2. Music

Following after every musical event may or may not be wise. As far as music is concerned, consider if the songs are simple or if they are concerned with appealing to the senses. Participating in extracurricular music activity, especially in a large singing group, isn't as easy without enrolment in a college, but there is always continued musical experience in other ways. In the psalms we are said to simply sing no matter what our circumstances. Psalm 9:11 says, "Sing praises to the LORD, which dwelleth in Zion: declare among the people his doings." Some people start their own little band in a local community. Perhaps you could participate or start one of your own. But in reality, the best place to expand musical participation is through a church. Develop better singing skills in a church. Develop better piano playing skills in a church. Develop better tuba playing skills in a church group. Some community groups would be open to godly music. Check to see if they are or not. You do not need to listen to the people who say one should go to a college to improve such musical skills. It is best to simply focus on music from an independent and non-complicated method of study. Participation in choir is a wonderful activity if there is choir available.

All in all, if you do not develop the habit of singing directly out of a hymn book and putting away worldly music, your Christian habits will not build strength! Consider the simple extra activity of singing for one hour a few days a week while picking up things, doing your laundry or other simple skills. Developing godly singing skills from home is a wonderful way to keep life joyful!

3. Art

Keeping a good hobby is enjoyable throughout life. However, beware of setting up art as an idol. Simply make it a pleasure to make life more enjoyable. Isa 45:20 states, "Assemble yourselves and come; draw near together, ye that are escaped of the nations: they have no knowledge that set up the wood of their graven image, and pray unto a god that cannot save." Perhaps you enjoy knitting. Perhaps you enjoy turning recycled material into something enjoyable. What about crafty writing and poetry. Keep these healthy hobbies going through the college years. Maybe there is a new hobby you would like to try like pottery. You don't have to create a special class to enjoy these arts, simply begin them. Homemaking in and of itself can also be an art. Sew some curtains, paints some paintings for a home. Needlework is a wonderful art. Whatever art activity you do as an extracurricular activity, make it enjoyable and not so intense as class material and study.

4. Social groups

On college campuses there are special social groups. Some are godly in their nature and some are terribly ungodly. As the bible says, Psalm 28:3 states, "Draw me not away with the wicked, and with the workers of iniquity, which speak peace to their neighbours, but mischief is in their hearts." This is the good thing about being an independent liberal arts bible college student. A person can choose to avoid these negative influences and social groups. Sadly, some of these social groups do show up on Christian college campuses. Perhaps there is a special community social group which seeks to help the poor in the community. Or another group that seeks to help single mothers. See if you would like to be a part of those social groups.   Overall, depending upon the size of your town, your social life will be filled to the full if you can participate in local library activity and local church activity. Participating in too much can make life more challenging. Take a note that church fellowship is not the same as a social group. Church fellowship should include bible study in some way. So to eliminate excess time and talk with people who are not interested in biblical things, may be to simply participate in church fellowship alone. However, some people find that being too focused on church and bible, can cause some issues, so the independent student should decide what works best for him or her. Always avoid social groups that are serving alcohol or encouraging ungodly behaviors. It is better to be among elderly women in your community who seek to preserve the community history than it is to be among college students who think themselves so wise as to constantly engage in riot activity.

5. Serving

There are many different ways to serve others. Maybe you may help others by helping repair sidewalks windows and other things that need repair in the community. Maybe you could put your name in the paper as a volunteer for any odd job. Being a part of a church can allow you to conquer various ways to serve others. Luke 22:26 says, "But ye shall not be so: but he that is greatest among you, let him be as the younger;

and he that is chief, as he that doth serve." Simply sign your name up for serving meal during church picnic. Join a prayer group or create one. Maybe you could sign up as a visitor of widows and elderly people who simply need a hand, a listening ear and do not have a lot of money to offer in return for your presence. Maybe you could serve by sewing for orphan or poor children in your community. The ways to serve during your free time are endless and offer a great way to grow spiritually. Because you are practicing bible study alongside secular studies, the ideas about who needs your care and serve seem to open up in many ways. Without a biblical guide, many people think of needy people as money and power, rather than simply people who need a listening ear and careful understanding.

Assignment:

1. List various extracurricular activities you would like to participate on a college campus. Try to find ways to participate in similar activities through your community.

2. Find ways to keep entertainment alive by choosing simple extra activities. Sing some hymns while doing the dishes, plant a flower for a neighbor and so forth.

Quiz:

 Evaluate your understanding of what was presented in this selection:

1. True/False A non-college student can participate in extra-curricular sporting events from a college.

2. True/False You do not have to sing hymns to find enjoyment in life.

3. Can art activities become an idol?

4. List various types of positive and negative social groups in your community. List the ways that they are positive or negative.

5. How can you serve others positively?

Genesis 21:2

For Sarah conceived, and bare Abraham a son in his old age, at the set time of which God had spoken to him.

Help Me I'm Busy, I'm Non-Traditional College Student. Time is Factor

1. Set up a book list

To enhance your ability to learn, you do not always need a college degree. In fact, all you would truly need to succeed in life is simply an education up until the eighth grade. Because of character problems in people and because some people simply do not communicate very well, education often continues well into post-secondary school. The spirit of God gives people understanding, Nehemiah 8:8 says, "So they read in the book in the law of God distinctly, and gave the sense, and caused them to understand the reading." However, if you have overcome your fears, have put a smile on your face, you too can educate yourself effectively and efficiently. If you have an education up until the eighth grade, all you would need is a solid book list which would include typical high school studies. The list of books should include 4 books relating to high school English, 4 books relating to high school math, 4 books related to high school science, and 4 books related to high school social studies or history. 4 additional books about various topics may also be discussed. Perhaps the subjects may be in art, music, physical fitness, agriculture, gardening, and any other subject matter a person would like to investigate. A person can read through each book in one year, while completing all questions and answers at the end of the chapters, adding additional books and assignments as you go. Set up the reading list to complete each book within one or two week's time. Before long a review or completion of high school will have been accomplished by the student. Perhaps one can take an ACT test or GED test to pass out of high school level exams, without all the hassle of enrolling in a public high school.

Furthermore, when a person would like to complete college level degree, but does not have ample time, simply create a 52 week book list. Perhaps a person has already started a career or has found themselves in a situation where they have started a family and cannot find a lot of time to themselves. Make a goal to read through each book within one week or less. Set aside one hour or more to read through each book. Maybe set aside another hour or two during the week to test, experiment, and write about and summarize each book read. Do not limit your skills in reading, simply because you are not enrolled in a college. Take up reading Count of Monte Cristo and other heavily detailed literatures. Read the good books, the popular books, the children's books, the books from other cultures and the bad books. Although, one should seriously consider avoiding the idea of putting romance novels or sensual materials on the reading list as these books are not there to enhance knowledge or spiritual growth.

2. Ensure Regular Bible study

All in all, if you do not have the opportunity to read a lot of other books, perhaps your life has found you filled with activity to the brim, or perhaps you have found more of your life reflects serving others in simple ways, if you have taken a lot of time to study bible, you are going to do well in this life. Set aside a special reading schedule that will allow you to carefully dive into the book of Ezekiel. 1Th 4:11 states, "And that ye study to be quiet, and to do your own business, and to work with your own hands, as we commanded you." Enhance your studies by following along with a special bible study guide. Keep pace with reading five psalms and one proverb chapter per day. As a result, your spirit will be filled to the brim, and you will know how to face the good and the bad in life, simply because you know what is inside of the book of Matthew. If you don't have a lot of time for the liberal arts portion of the college degree, if you can focus on enhancing your knowledge in the bible alone, you will do well. Focus on enhancing skills in speaking the bible effectively, focus on enhancing overcoming of fears, focus on overcoming fear of not knowing the meaning of certain words and meanings within the bible. When you know what righteousness means and have memorized such verses, you will get a good solid bible college degree, simply by choosing to memorize and deeply studying portions of the bible. A good outline of character improvements that occur because of bible study is a good thing to have on hand.

3. Blocks of time

Face the reality that life on earth requires time. In biblical time, there is reference to heavenly orders in regards to time, Gen 17:21 states, "But my covenant will I establish with Isaac, which Sarah shall bear unto thee at this set time in the next year." Time wasted is perhaps time used to mock or scorn rather than to learn how to rid one's self of these unusual terrible self-driven desires. Make sure to set aside time to read the books that will enhance your knowledge in such a way that you can adequately defend biblical truth in a world full of error. Setting aside one hour a day for reading apologetic writings and history of Christian persecution can majorly enhance your ability to give back what you have been given in your freedom to study bible in the first place. Perhaps on the Sabbath (note: this book is for all denominations and Christian beliefs), you could spend extra time reading exclusively godly books and literature which encourages you towards more holy living. You may, as a result, find such studies reflect your work and enhancement in your community. By prayer and supplication, your life becomes transformed to good works which enable extensive spiritual growth. Along with setting aside one special day and an hour a day to read books, setting aside a special holiday week or two once in the fall and once in the spring, can also greatly enhance your ability to reflect on bible and on good books that enhance positive qualities in your life.

4. Teach children along with study

Due to raising family, some mothers and fathers neglect studies and seek to devour themselves in selfish or addictive behavior, rather than demonstrating godly behavior to their children. Just because a person has children, does not mean he or she should allow their children to make bad choices. Heb 12:9 proclaims, "Furthermore we have had fathers of our flesh which corrected us, and we gave them reverence: shall we not much rather be in subjection unto the Father of spirits, and live?"   Rather, the children should be incorporated into the studies. If a certain passage of bible is being studied by the adult parent in the family, the accommodating bible story at a child's level should also be included. For children beginning to read, or fully capable of reading, the child should be encouraged to read the bible portion the adult parent is also reading. This enhances family togetherness and understanding. Even if the adult is studying advanced literature of some other sort, the parent should encourage the child to study small portions of the advanced literature as well. There is no reason children should not be included in enhanced or advanced studies, even if those studies involve study of the planet Mars. Children learn many things quite well, if they find those things to be interesting.

Assignment:

1. Write out two or more 52 week reading lists. Include a variety of books, even books you would enjoy for entertainment. Make sure the books are not dirty or consuming of your time.

2. Evaluate your time. Schedule in proper bible study times in your home.

Quiz:

Evaluate your understanding of what was presented in this selection:

1. True/False People who have college degrees are always wiser than those who do not have college degrees.

2. How much time each day should a busy person set aside to study?

3. Is it possible to be content in only study of the bible?

4. Do you actually have a lot of time on earth to study?

5. How can an adult incorporate bible study for children while the adult is studying biblical topics?

Leviticus 10:11

And that ye may teach the children of Israel all the statutes which the LORD hath spoken unto them by the hand of Moses.

Home Education? Along with College Level Study?

1. Age 0-7

When teaching and working with children that are between the ages of 0-7, consider that it is never too early to start getting a child interested in reading. Mat 18:3 says, "And said, Verily I say unto you, Except ye be converted, and become as little children, ye shall not enter into the kingdom of heaven." Force when reading and excessive testing should never be done to young children. Even schools that do this are not encouraging children towards more imaginative or creative living, but rather towards excess of educational idolatry. Set aside about 1/2 hour each day to instruct young children in some way or another. Simply reading from psalms and proverbs can help stimulate much mental capacity in the young children. Point to the heart when the bible mentions heart. Early reading books that encourage reading can begin as soon as the child shows interest in sitting still. Once good reading habits begin, then introduction to bible can begin as well.

A young child may study along with what a parent is studying in secular world-view. He or she can join in a cooking activity or gardening activity quite easily. The child may also play "repeat after me" games if the parent is studying the geographic landscape of Antarctica or Vector Calculus. Simply state the problem, have the child repeat after the parent and have the child point to the various aspects and details the parent is learning.

Often parents of today are finding that the Montessori methods of teaching are perfect for young children to absorb different skills. Study these methods of learning. There are other methods of study too. Consider keeping a separate shoe-box or tote box filled with various instructional items. During free time or whenever the parent is a little busy, keep the child learning by exposing the child to various items. Consider purchasing items to fill these boxes by finding the items free, used or at cheap dollar stores. Include any of the following boxes among learning supply and rotate by each day of the month: 1. Nature Box (Pine Cones, Rocks etc) 2. Dress-up Box (fabric, hats, old shirts etc) 3. Phonics Books Box 4. Alphabet Box 5. Math Box 6. Sewing Box 7. Music Box (Note Names, Pictures of Instruments, Pictures of Composers etc) 8. Paint Box 9. Pictures Box (Magazine Clippings, Calendars, Photos) 10. Memories Box (Diary of events in child's life, scrap books, pictures of events) 11. Maps Box (Local, Parks, World Maps) 12. Office Box (Stamps, paper clips etc) 13. Instruments Box (Harmonica, rattles, drums etc) 14. Art Box (Crayons, paper scraps, tissue paper, beads etc) 15. Egg Carton Box (ideas for crafts with egg cartons) 16. Bubble Wrap (keep busy popping bubble wrap) 17. Character Box (Focus on good behavior) 18. Culture Box (Faces from difference places) 19. History Box (Timelines encyclopedia article clippings) 20. Bells and Whistles Box (different types of bells, whistle things) 21. Ball and Paddle Box (any type of ball and a few ping pong paddles) 22. Cars Box (All types of cars and ramps for cars) 23. Clocks Box (watches, winding things, timers) 24. Stencils Box 25. Coloring books box 26. Bubbles and Bathtub Box 27. Hardware Box (Nails, screws, hammers, pipes, wires) 28. Etiquette and Table Box (Set table neatly, fancy introductions) 29. Board Books Box (Different types and sizes) 30. Bible box (Flash cards, games, books bible stories etc) 31. You choose Topic Box.

During the young years, if you are able, definitely avoid allowing the child to use computer as a way to pass time. Even 1/2 an hour of watching a screen seems to have negative rather than positive impact on a young developing brain. Plan to keep computers away from the child until the child can safely choose to stay focused on only good instructional internet video or games. A wise home will not have internet access. Along with considering the early years, much focus should be on character and behavior, rather than on reading and writing. A child who joyfully helps clean a bathroom is better in the long run than a child who can recite the names of all planets in its various details in our solar system. A good child training book will encourage disciplined Christian aspects of education over allowing the child to do whatever he or she wants all the time. Furthermore, children should also be encouraged towards basic etiquette and grooming. Please and thank you, respect and praise should be encouraged in the child. Cleaning up one's own mess, attaining clean clothes and clean hands should be encouraged. Though, if the child is not perfect in these things, do not worry too heavily. Eventually the child will find cleanliness to be more enjoyable than sloppy disrespectful living. It does not take a lot of money or knowledge to teach the child to remain clean.

2. Age 7-10

By the time the child is seven, he or she should be able to confidently pick up a bible and read several verses. Jesus wants little children to come to him. Mar 10:14 says, "But when Jesus saw it, he was much displeased, and said unto them, Suffer the little children to come unto me, and forbid them not: for of such is the kingdom of God." He or she may stumble across a few words until they are closer to nine years old, but he or she should be capable of forming out the sounds of those words. A good collection of McGuffey Readers and other classical literatures can help overcome that burden. If the parent is studying while teaching the child to read, the parent may find it useful to read classical literature to the child. Reading a bible in and of itself is very educational for the child from age 7-10. By the time the child has reached the age of 10, he or she should be fully capable of reading the bible independently along with the parent. Though, do not force bible reading on the child, rather just encourage the habit of bible verse memorization and meditation on psalms and proverbs or other passages. Once again, like the 0-7 age group, do not force reading skills yet at this stage. The child's eyes are still developing.

The child who is 7-10 may begin writing effectively. By the time the child has reached the age of 8, all the letters of the alphabet should be written neatly and quickly by the child. Cursive writing can begin any time after age 8. Start by writing one lowercase cursive letter. Then write the capital letter along with one cursive word. After the child can effectively write cursive words, have the child write a few sentences in cursive. Write whatever the parent is studying or write whatever is being studied in the bible at the time. The more the child can practice writing the better. Include in the writing practice a little spelling as well. Be sure to include biblical based spelling words. Pick out words that are

4-8 letters long and have the child spell those. Along with spelling, consider little grammar skills as well. Get a classic grammar book for children and point out the aspects of grammar found in bible passages. Point to the verbs, nouns and other parts of speech. This will cut out on a lot of extra time otherwise spent away from bible study.

Math skills should be practiced with classical literature like Ray's Arithmetic, or may be practiced alongside what a parent is learning. If the parent is doing experiments with plants, have the child learn to measure and test the plants along with the parent. Expose the child to the numbers of legs on insects, numbers of wings on birds and other natural things. When reading bible, study each natural thing mentioned and determine how may legs, stars, wings and other conditions God gave to these things. Even when parts of the body are mentioned in the bible, study how many heart beats occur in a minute and how many bones are in the hand. Numbers are a part of nature and a part of life.

When the parent is studying a secular subject, the child may keep notebook pages of what is being learned. If the parent is studying Music, the child student may draw pictures of Mozart as a child learning to play the piano. Drawing a diagram of an ancient castle may also be a way for the child to learn along with the parent as the parent completes learning activities. By being an active learner, the child will not be far behind with the parent who is also learning new things about this world.

3. Age 11-14

By the time the child reaches the age of fourteen, he or she should have a pretty solid understanding of the bible, unless he or she grew up in an environment where bible reading was forbidden or other issues with religious freedom restrictions. Mar 10:15 states, "Verily I say unto you, Whosoever shall not receive the kingdom of God as a little child, he shall not enter therein." The child of age 11-14 can participate in reading a full chapter of psalms and proverbs each day. He or she may also read one chapter in Law, one chapter in Old Testament, one chapter in Gospel and one chapter in New Testament each week. The child who is encouraged towards comprehension and bible verse meditation will do better in the long run, than a child left to himself to understand the bible. Overall, if the child is not reading about three chapters a day along with the adult, and deciding to meditate on the pages of scripture, he or she simply may not be exposed to bible enough. Other entertainments may be in mind for the child under age 14. It is up to the parent to decide how he or she would like to manage the child's heart in that way. It is not up to a church denomination, school practice or other things in life to influence these lifestyle decisions.

The child aged 11-14 will advance their reading, by reading along with the parent in their advanced reading materials and along with special reading books that help the child advance in comprehension and reading skills. Words and ideas not found in the bible should be encouraged in reading skills, because many old literatures used ideas advanced from the bible and beyond those ideas. A child who cannot understand classic literature, will be a basic child who simply will not use or need such reasoning. Most people typically read at an eighth grade level and never really use more advanced literature than that for the rest of their lives. The KJV Holy Bible is written at about a fifth grade level, but the words and phrases within, sometimes give advanced literature exposures.

If the child picked up on basic addition, subtraction, multiplication, division during age 10 and under, it is ok delay math skills lightly to see the child advance to algebra level quickly and efficiently during the 11-14 year level. Much time and energy in math principles can actually be delayed slightly until the child is more dedicated to independent studies. When the child is older, math computations come much easier for the child.

Hand writing should be quick and efficient for the 11-14 year old child. He or she should be capable of writing out entire pages of literature in cursive if asked to do so. Hand written material should be neat enough to be legible and diligently careful enough to be reproduced as an art work.

A child of 11-14 years old should have a good general knowledge of science material, history material, culture material and other basic skills that help the child to know how to deal with the various issues in life. Notebook pages help the parent and child work together to ensure enough knowledge is acquired. Little tests and quizzes can ensure that the child is learning quite well. A fourteen year old should be capable of completing similar studies as the parent or similar accumulation of knowledge as that of a college student, but without so much pressure for accuracy. Simply attain a general knowledge in the fourteen year old.

Grammar and spelling should be sufficient enough so that the child of fourteen can recall definitions for all the words in a KJV Holy Bible. Any word from prudence to diligence should have meaning for the 14 year old child. Spelling should also be computed well enough that the 14 year old child can spell accurately all words found in the KJV Holy Bible.

Any less than that, and the child will not be able to complete high school or will fall short in college education. Perhaps, without the ability to study KJV vocabulary and spelling, the child will believe he or she can be educated without the need for bible or vice versa without the need for further study. If the child knows he needs to learn more in a certain area, he or she will be open to wisdom and knowledge beyond the eighth grade level.

4. Age 14-18

It is optional for the student to continue with studies up until age 18. In fact, if the child is skilled in many areas, he or she will not need skills past the age of 18 to survive! Many people live off of an eighth grade education. However, due to the problem of bad habits and bad character in the person, it is better to continue education, than to remain seated in Inactive roles in life! As the bible says, Mar 10:18, "And Jesus said unto him, Why callest thou me good? there is none good but one, that is, God."

The person who is 14-18 years old should be able to care for a household for 2 weeks alone, without constant supervision from an adult. Some youth become nurse's helpers at this age. Others start up their own farmer's market business at this age. It will depend on the dedication and time the young student would like to put into something. Overall, it is best to avoid gaining so many skills in areas that will not assist in workable skills. Skills in basketball may or may not be needed unless one want to become a physical fitness teacher.

Bible knowledge should increase at this age, in such a way that the student has the habit of reading the minimum of 3 chapters of bible per day. If the child has not repented of his or her sin by this stage in life, all the bible study will not be effective. It will be draining and not effective. However, the student should continue with the studies that the parent conducts anyhow, until he or she is living on his or her own.

Overall subject matter should be included in such a way that the child knows all that he or she can know about Mozart and Plato, China and the Tower of Pisa. Intense detailed college level studies are not necessary, but it is possible to begin intense knowledge acquisition at any time between ages 14-19.

Reading, grammar, writing and spelling skills can still be enhanced in the age of 14-18. Increase the intensity of the books read. Be sure to include godly books and character based books among the books selections. Godly books will enhance the furtherance of the gospel for the 14-18 year old child. Do not be afraid to introduce pre-marriage or home ideas books at this stage in life. Some children feel they are ready to be married at the young age of 16! Even if a child chooses young marriage, be sure to encourage the enhancement of education beyond the high school level, because many frustrations and anger people face in life are simply because they did not know how to handle such situations.

Mathematics is typically only used at an algebra level in may careers and professions. Do not avoid the intense math and science classes as they may be useful for the child's future career. If the parent is studying advance mathematic skills, encourage the child to practice the same math problems. Accounting, economics and carpentry all use mathematics skills, so be sure to include these in the 14-18 year old child's high school classes.

All in all, a child may choose any route he or she feels is the best in accomplishing a full high school level education. He or she may choose to read a set number of books that cover several different topics as well as practice writing, and other accompanying skills. The child may choose to use an actual high school level curriculum from an internet resource to obtain a GED. Otherwise the child should be encouraged to incorporate much bible study into his or her studies as the bible will remain forever and should be an everyday part of the child's life. Do not force the resistant child to read the bible constantly, however, simply wait until the child is ready to participate. Overall, the high school level student should be able to accomplish mini versions of college level "liberal arts bible college" classes.

Assignment:

1. Create a little preschool and nursery school curriculum to practice daily and weekly activity. Fill in ideas for singing songs, exploring nature and so forth.

2. Try to teach at a local church to the youth. If no youth are available at a church, volunteer at a local school. Be a tutor that helps young children learn to read.

Quiz:

Evaluate your understanding of what was presented in this selection:

1. How may a bible be used and read to a young person to make it expressive?

2. Should you read the bible to the youth in a boring manner?

3. List ways that the youth can learn to read and write using a bible.

4. Should you ever force bible meditation and reading on a child?

5. At what grade level can people function in life and thrive especially if they know the scripture fairly well? Why is work ethic and character more important than knowing a lot of things? (Knowledge in and of itself is not bad)

Deuteronomy 4:1

Now therefore hearken, O Israel, unto the statutes and unto the judgments, which I teach you, for to do them, that ye may live, and go in and possess the land which the LORD God of your fathers giveth you.

Senior Paper or Project

1. Written work and presentation

After you have completed a set number of credits, you may write a senior paper illustrating your understanding. An average independent class should be three to four credits. In the bible written words are given for God's glory. Ezekiel 9:3 indicates, "And the glory of the God of Israel was gone up from the cherub, whereupon he was, to the threshold of the house. And he called to the man clothed with linen, which had the writer's inkhorn by his side;" Accumulating work should be 12 credits or more per semester and a total of 96 credits. For the "bible book major" the classes should fit in to a set of 64 credits or 16 total classes related to the book major. As it is rather unusual for a student to major in the book of Obadiah, it is even more unusual to find a non-Christian choosing to major in the book of Obadiah in the first place. Majoring in a book of the bible simply exemplifies a complete understanding of one particular book of the bible along with understanding of major elements of human life.

To illustrate full understanding of the book of Obadiah, for example, a written report should be accomplished to show great understanding in this area. Perhaps the written work could be exemplifying a particular aspect of how this book can be applied to regular life. Paper topics could include anything like the following: "A Look at Obadiah and the Amplification of Small Community Accomplishments," or "The Elderly and their Appreciation of Principles Taken from the Book of Obadiah," or something unusual "The Robin, the Rooster and Bird Life Arranged Around Principles in the Book of Obadiah," or "Bach, an Orchestra and Obadiah" or "The Vector Calculus Principles of the Book of Obadiah." Such written work would and should be quite educational in nature. It would also illustrate usefulness for everyday life.

As a person accomplishes a written piece, it would also be appreciative to present what was learned as well during the four years of study. Perhaps a local library is willing to open its doors to your presentation. Perhaps a church is willing to have a coffee hour while listening to a simple presentation about your studies. Many elderly people are interested in learning something new, they would be glad to hear that a person can still use biblical literature in an informative way. The presentation itself should be about ten to twenty minutes in length. Perhaps, if you have developed other talents as well in your studies, you can include a little musical arrangement, art presentation as well. The more you show that you can accomplish much in independent college studies, the more people would be interested in your work.

2. Publishing a piece of work

One way to ensure that you have a full understanding of the goals in developing a "Liberal Arts Bible College Major," is to publish what you have learned in the form of a book. You may write about biblical topics, other topics or a combination of both. The bible itself is meant to be published in all nations in the globe! Mar 13:10 illustrates clearly, "And the gospel must first be published among all nations." You do not need to use a major publishing company, though you may still decide to do so. With the availability of the internet and computers, it is easier than ever to self-publish materials. However, beware of the task in self-publishing without editing or making your work look professional. E-books are a dime a dozen. Simple little e-book instruction manuals can be found at any farmer's market. This doesn't show your uniqueness in study of a book of the bible. All in all, the published material should be useful, appealing and show examples of how your four years of study provided you with much skills, knowledge and wisdom.

3. Compilation of information about my classes and accomplishments

Before you begin creating your classes, make sure you have a special record book that allows you to make good decisions about the directions in education. Include your homemade college course catalog, locations for resources you received your information and any other information about your independent college. Even if you don't complete a class or feel as if you are failing at a class, keep these records.

Keep all tests, papers and quizzes. Keep all presentations, projects and activities. The more records that are taken and the more goals you achieve, the more success you will have in keeping a proper portfolio. Keeping a reading list and written summaries of what you have read can show that you are fully capable of reading multiple different authors and reading from a variety of different people in different backgrounds and lifestyles.

Even presenting a written record of what you have read in the bible and what you have memorized, can help people see how you are investing your time in not only liberal arts, but also in bible study. Keep track of these things will help you for the rest of your life as it shows you are attaining bible study habits.

When you have a quality portfolio, you can show any future employer or you can show any future customer at your business of your understanding and knowledge. The bible itself bears its record which many men seek, John 1:34 says, "And I saw, and bare record that this is the Son of God." Perhaps you need to work with a bank or a lawyer, when you can prove that you have studied at college level and in an independent manner, you will get more credibility with what you know. Your local library will get much use out of all of your studies, and many of its books that have been gaining dust will suddenly be opened due to your simple desire to attain an "independent college degree."

Assignment:

1. Locate places where publishing a book can take place. Look on the internet and find resources.

2. Get a binder, file box, manila folders, organizers and whatever else is needed to sort information that displays a desire to study in God's word as well as gain general knowledge. Use laminators and page protectors to preserve important documents and papers.

Quiz:

Evaluate your understanding of what was presented in this selection:

1. How may a student display, present and identify understanding in their college degree without the use of a college?

2. What types of titles may you give a senior presentation?

3. Why is publishing a book a good way to demonstrate understanding?

4. What types of records should you keep?

5. What types of people would be interested in viewing your portfolio and information about what you have completed in studies?

2 Corinthians 10:10

For his letters, say they, are weighty and powerful; but his bodily presence is weak, and his speech contemptible.

Completion with a Ceremony, Diploma and Certificate

1. The end shows growth from the beginning

Before the student begins study he or she should notice that he or she needed improvement in various areas of study. Music, Health, Nature, History-Culture-Geography, Language, Math according to bible and nature, and overall Character should improve due to enhanced biblical studies. Exodus 35:31 emphasizes spiritual growth along with other areas of growth, "And he hath filled him with the spirit of God, in wisdom, in understanding, and in knowledge, and in all manner of workmanship." The study of music should focus more dutifully on godly hymns and perhaps classical musical works that revolve around such principles. The study of math should cause the student to compute equations more effectively and efficiently understand coordination with biblical principles and natural principles. The study of language should cause the student to improve his speaking skills, writing skills and to make more godly choices, and languages use that directs readers to godly living. Overall character should be improved in such a way that fears are overcome, changes are made in impact in the community and surrounding area. The study of the bible along with strengthening wisdom and knowledge in various areas will help the independent student to succeed in what he or she does with time and energy while here on earth. Evil cannot dwell with good, so the strengths of good in knowledge should outshine the bad.

2. All goals accomplished

As the classes are created, all tasks should be completed efficiently and effectively. The process of memorization should have occurred in such a way that an individual notices the changes in his or her knowledge. Records of these goals and the accomplishments should be recorded to show what areas need improvement and what areas need reduction in study and what areas need enhancement in study. Be aware that you will not be able to study everything but you should study many things. Ecclesiastes 12:12 says, "And further, by these, my son, be admonished: of making many books there is no end; and much study is a weariness of the flesh." Perhaps a change in method of study can help enhance the quality of the test scores. Do not abandon study of a certain area of study if it appears that a student can only accomplish a C or even D grade in various tests and quizzes! Rather, seek ways to improve study and enhance time spent in study in this area. Seek a tutor from a college or through internet resource if needed. Giving up is not good for the life of the student. Seek to achieve goals big and goals small. Seek the challenges. Seek the impossible. Seek deepness in bible study and character improvement overall.

3. Invitation to a ceremony?

Did you achieve your goals? Were your goals high enough so that they were challenging to your mind and your spiritual growth? Maybe you could establish a special awards ceremony. In God's word people were encouraged to rejoice in godly works. Deuteronomy 30:9 specifies, "And the LORD thy God will make thee plenteous in every work of thine hand, in the fruit of thy body, and in the fruit of thy cattle, and in the fruit of thy land, for good: for the LORD will again rejoice over thee for good, as he rejoiced over thy fathers." Would a church be willing to sponsor your ceremony? Would a group of nursing home residents be happy to attend your awards ceremony? What about a special group that serves homeless people or disadvantaged poor people in your neighborhood? Invite family friends and other people who support you in your efforts towards independent college degree! Maybe you could give a 15 minute presentation, display or other method of showing the knowledge you have acquired during your four years of independent study, and then immediately afterwards have a small awards ceremony! Perhaps a group of people in your area are a part of this journey to major in an actual book of the bible!

4. Majored in the book of Obadiah...now what?

When a student gives much study to the book of Obadiah and perhaps a couple other books in the bible, the world looks at such a major and says, that such studies were not useful. However, little did they know that there is much power and word knowledge in the bible, so they will not have the knowledge you have? Ancient knowledge that never fails man-kind! When presenting to an employer that your major in college which you listed was "Obadiah, Jonah and Micah" while the title of your academy was Independent Study at Glory Academy, you should have records ready to prove that you were an actual student! However, if you are going to work with wicked employer who dislikes Christian beliefs, Rom 8:18 states, "For I reckon that the sufferings of this present time are not worthy to be compared with the glory which shall be revealed in us," you may simply list, Independent Study in various fields with majority study in "human rights and awareness." It is up to you whether you would like to present your biblical studies to wicked employers and you happen to be working in an area where Christian persecution is prevalent.

In some cases, if you do well enough with recording what you have learned, a graduate school post-secondary school may encourage you to design your "major" in the biblical topics to be appealing to graduate and other professional schools. Some post-secondary colleges love to work with independent major and minor studies. In many cases, it is actually best for Christians to remain humble in their behavior and simply work with what they are given. Some simply choose to wash dishes at a favorite small town family diner! God will provide in all cases!

Assignment:

1. List areas where you need to improve. Set goals in each of those areas. See if your studies lead to improve in those areas.

2. List places where you may hold an awards ceremony. List various people who may sponsor you.

Quiz:

Evaluate your understanding of what was presented in this selection:

1. List the various areas of study that enhance your skills in this world.

2. Are all students able to study everything they could possibly know?

3. What types of people could you invite to an awards ceremony?

4. What type of way should you list reference to your abilities as an "independent student" towards one who is not discriminatory to biblical thinking?

5. What type of way should you list reference to your abilities as an "independent student" towards one who is discriminatory to biblical thinking?

John 7:15

And the Jews marvelled, saying, How knoweth this man letters, having never learned?

Setting up a Mini College

1. One class costs no more than five loaves of bread

Consider that the cost of education runs high. It is so high that for some colleges, the student is required to pay the sum of the cost for an entire small house, each year! Such loans are a drain and a burden to the college student. It is imaginative nonsense to believe a government will properly pay for good quality classes. It would be anti-Christian and anti-biblical to believe that the world should pay for the poor student to attend colleges in order for the student to fully succeed in life. Exodus 23:3 states, "Neither shalt thou countenance a poor man in his cause." Taxation is stealing from the widow and the orphan in many cases. So it is not good to promote high costs for college classes especially if Christians believe they "need" such classes.

How can the cost for a college where students literally major in a book of the bible be lowered to the cost of five loaves of bread? Simple. The students that attend such colleges are "independent students." The overseer helps the student ensure that his studies are effective! He makes sure that the student is reading enough materials and covering enough questions to ensure thorough evaluations of what is being studied. The cost for five loaves of bread will simply go to the cost for the overseer to evaluate the quality of the student's goals and studies.

If the cost runs higher than five loaves of bread, then the student is no longer an "independent student" in his or her studies. He or she has chosen to be just like regular college students. The classes will no longer have biblical themes, but could run into secularizing the bible. Other than a basic overview of the Bible class, the majority of the classes would encourage thought about verses from the bible in comparison to secular knowledge.

2. Book of the Bible titled class and comparisons to accreditation.

Perhaps one college could focus only on certain themes of study. Another college could focus on study based on denomination principles. Yet another college could focus on a small amount of topic classes, leaving the student to explore other areas on his or her own. All in all the focus and major in these colleges should always be to major in actual books of the bible, which is what a non-Christian would not want and to make such classes entirely affordable to the poor and disadvantaged! It is un-Christ-like to call people to a college, yet to leave students with such disgraceful amounts of debt! Even if that college is specifically designed to help people understand basic principles of the bible and encourage pastors or ministers to improve their understanding of humanity. More specifically, it is such a disgrace to our heavenly father to offer classes in "accounting" or "sociology" to a financially superior or advantaged non-Christian who hates scripture, will not obey scripture, hates families who raise their children with biblical understanding and to give such a degree to a person who has no interest in bible from a college that calls itself supportive of Christian principles or considers itself a Christian college. The bible concludes that there are weeds among the wheat even among households and can apply to Christian colleges as well. Mat 10:36 indicates, "And a man's foes shall be they of his own household." That is a very disgraceful misunderstanding of the principles of scripture in the first place. Beware of allowing such weeds to invade the mind and heart of Christian or biblical based colleges. Such weeds eventually spill out into communities and how they function as a whole in mind and heart as well!

How are classes to be compared to accreditation classes? Simply study how the accreditation process of colleges works. How does the secular world evaluate the difficulty of a class? A set number of pages can help determine if enough content will be covered in the class. The difficulty in the vocabulary will help determine if the class is suitable for certain people of intellectual gift and ability. All in all, if the classes that are developed by an independent student show that the student is serious in his studies and growth, his or her ability to make impact in the secular world will be enhanced by such growth in knowledge and wisdom. The unfortunate thing is that accreditation takes away the biblical approach to knowledge and wisdom. It also causes the classes to increase in cost! Even if the knowledge established by the independent student is superior to the general student, his or her wisdom will not be seen as valuable to an employer unless he or she can claim and prove that it is comparable. This is the risk that a bible college liberal arts student should be willing to take. His or her knowledge should be enhanced enough so that he or she could enter a graduate school, medical school or law school if they would like to, in the completion of basic independent studies. Perhaps in the near future, through prayer and determination, a BIBLE BASED accreditation process can be established. It would outline the quality of the class, the necessity of the class for enhancement of biblical and fine Christian literature or knowledge. After all, the apostle Paul had in comparison to today, the equivalent of three Master's Degrees! Christians should not fear knowledge itself!

3. A provision for housing

If a group of people or a certain church would like to set up a mini college, perhaps that mini-college could set up an affordable provision for housing. The unfortunate thing with housing for college students is that some of the college students are not serious students of the bible, hence hearts and minds get skewed jargon and information! To ensure that this problem is resolved, make sure that each student indicates what he or she is studying each day in the bible and shows evidence of such study! Furthermore, also consider offering a camp-ground style housing for students. Consider carefully how to set up the shelters and meeting places, even if they are simple and are easily adjusted to weather conditions. Pro 31:21 states, "She is not afraid of the snow for her household: for all her household are clothed with scarlet." This reduces the cost for electrical appliances and other bells and whistles which are only best for the home-owner or settled person. Students may even choose to build their own mini cabin! It is simple to do and can be done with as little as one weekend and some careful planning. The student can then sell or take his or her cabin home when he is done with registration at the mini-college. It is easier to set up housing for students in country side where very little regulation occurs for housing of youth from age 16-24. Basic knowledge of morality is all that is essential in country life.

Housing in the city life may be possible if people of greater financial benefit choose to buy or rent a large business space and change it into a special housing unit specifically for college students. Maybe a space between a craft store and jewelry store could make a decent housing unit. Of course it would be a space for housing and not an actual apartment. If there are city codes restricting the establishment of student housing, be sure to pay attention to those specific codes. Each student will need to find a way to pay a portion of the rent price for the space. All in all, it is best to set aside a portion of cost for an actual bunk, dormitory, or apartment size sleeping spaces if a church group or group of people choose to set up a college living space for "independent liberal arts bible study" students. Typically 4 students can stay in a two bedroom apartment. This reduces cost and gives the student more time away from working and more focus on study. Also, there is a possibility that an entire home may be purchased, solely for the purpose of allowing independent bible students to study and grow in their knowledge and grace.

4. A church group accumulates knowledge and references

When a church group has a place to gather, that church group can find a place to store special books from which to educate students and any other curious adults. Records of many things are kept In many books and methods of keeping track of human history and natural history. Rev 20:12 says, "And I saw the dead, small and great, stand before God; and the books were opened: and another book was opened, which is the book of life: and the dead were judged out of those things which were written in the books, according to their works." Of course, there may be something where the church group decides not to include books that are negative in nature among their stacks of literature. Sharing books among a church group is a wonderful idea. Not only should such positive literature be found in the stacks of books, but perhaps a special book club can be established among the church group. When church groups find positive leadership role models, the church group helps expand faith in biblical topics and in how to deal with the secular world. Perhaps the church group could find special speakers to come and speak on certain topics. Books of value can be related to cooking and cleaning, or they can be related to study of astronomy and cultures in Africa. It all depends on how the church group would like to approach situations. All in all it is very beneficial to include classical post-copyright literatures among the collection of books. Such literature shows the "old paths" of life. This helps women and men learn how to function in life without so much struggle and strife against ungodly ideologies in our modern era.

5. Regulations of dress code, conduct and so on.

Among the church group, there may be a special dress code. Are women required to wear dresses that are the length of the calves and cover the upper arm? Are women required to wear a head covering? What about men? Are they not allowed to wear flashy t-shirts? Even t-shirts that promote any sort of Christian trend? Conduct. 1Ti 2:9 indicates, "In like manner also, that women adorn themselves in modest apparel, with shamefacedness and sobriety; not with broided hair, or gold, or pearls, or costly array." Are the men and women in the college forbidden from dating unless a betrothal is in mind? Are courtships to be determined through parental guidance? Are betrothals to occur only after holy-spirit guidance? Perhaps it is more of a relaxed atmosphere, but with more focus on the heart as guide. Are students forbidden from listening to "Christian Rock" or from watching "Christian Movies"? Are they discouraged from eating processed foods? On the questionnaire, are students asked if they love the church they grew up within? Are they asked if they love to serve disabled people? Are they encouraged to only attend worship on certain days and times? Are students encouraged to reduce electrical appliance usage? Keep these things in mind, if a mini-college with independent students is established. Each denomination has various goals and traditions that work in keeping students and adults attuned to the bible more effectively.

6. Scheduling time for study and time for recreation.

As a mini-college or independent studies based college, schedule times for worship and fellowship should be the priority as promotion of biblical themes. Perhaps this specific college has certain elements of study which each student should study within the bible in order to succeed in their bible college portion of study. Perhaps this specific college has certain books which each student should read as part of their curriculum. Be sure to allow the students to schedule their times for study of these materials. Does this mini-college include a time for singing? Does this college of independent students include times for students to participate in a road trip to go rock-climbing. The bible encourages order. 1Co 14:40 says, "Let all things be done decently and in order." What about scheduling a time to visit elderly folks at a local nursing home. All in all, the college should allow enough time to bible studies in the classes as well as studies of the materials presented. The college should include that it encourages lots of bible study times and at specific times, to help students grow in biblical studies habits. Perhaps the college sets aside Torah or Law studies in the morning, Old Testament Studies in the afternoon, Gospel studies in the early evening and finally New Testament studies in the late evening. Prayer times could be included in these times as well. Maybe this specific college has a healing ministry for people who were once involved with wicked things in life, like drugs, sexual impurity, terrorism or any other negative influence. Each college should determine how it would like to set up times for study, faith practices and recreation and to allow the student to balance such things in life. Each college should encourage the student in a major that focuses on a book of the bible.

Assignment:

1. For those interested: Design a college. Include required classes, conduct codes, where you will keep records for your college and so forth. Decide if it will include many students or simply a few. Decide if you will hire actual professors or not.

2. For those interested: Choose a method of developing a college from scratch. Start a college out of an old farm shed. Perhaps you can develop a college that features special bible book classes for those interested in furthering their education.

Quiz:

Evaluate your understanding of what was presented in this selection:

1. Should bible based classes cost more than a few loaves of bread? Why or why not?

2. How may a person compare a book of the bible based class to accreditation scores?

3. How can a mini college provide housing?

4. Does a college need regulations? What types of regulations?

5. What significant features may a church group or denomination provide for a college?

John 7:16

Jesus answered them, and said, My doctrine is not mine, but his that sent me.

Conclusion

1. Effective bible study habits

The overall goal in post-secondary education should be to develop bible study habits! Without that ability, students fall prey to many manipulative theories and ideas that hold no place in the reality of Christ's kingdom! There may even be manipulative ideas that come out of a specific conservative Christian denomination due to jargon and other non-essential conversations. Not that conservative biblical groups are bad because of this effect, but rather it shows the increased need for bible study. When the youth have established bible study skills, it becomes essentially easier to deal with the ups and downs of life in accordance of how "the word" fills human lives with greatness and goodness. The more one can sense what the bible actually says vs. what people think it says, the stronger the faith becomes! Much meditation and study of the word gives effectual and fervent value to the Christian believer!

2. Willingness to try new learning techniques and skills

A good student is a student who is willing to listen! He is not overcome
with so much pride that he believes he or she is always right just
because he or she has fully studied the bible through several different
times. No, it is more than that. One must be willing to read new books,
try new skills and see life from a different angle! Yes, there is a simple
living aspect to life and even expression of the bible, in such a way that
a person can simply walk to and from the local church group, live
without electricity in one's home in the community and just assume
basics of life come from one's own grocery store as well as assume that
the best conversations come from the local library, but in reality, there
is more learning that should grow and continue in the life of a bible
believer. When in the youth, it is easier to challenge the mind to grasp
new concepts. It is easier to learn Hebrew or Greek before reaching the
age of 50. It is good for the growth in understanding of music to learn
to play Bach and practice etiquette skills for formal dining. It is good to
learn how to improve speaking skills so that an audience can
understand fully what you are trying to communicate. To be unique in
the eyes of creator is essential to spiritual reality. Overall, it is good to
learn how to work with disabled people in a more humble and kind
manner! Various issues can show up in life, and various skills and
talents are needed in life, so it is essentially good to gain knowledge in
various arts and sciences!

3. Positive character growth...

The effect of study habits in both biblical and secular topics should lead
to positive character growth. Were you once constantly angry at certain
people? Maybe you constantly disliked people close to you. Did you

once dislike a certain group of people? What about fear of certain things or people? Are you afraid of being alone in this world, or do you know the savior who is always with you? These things will explain the quality of your character. The more you recognize the negative effects sin has had on our life, the more your character will improve with the help and aide of bible study. If you are interested in studies in astronomy or in the arts, you can freely do so as an independent student. Perhaps your studies will be sufficient enough to provide ample information to a college or researching center itself! You never know what you can discover by independent study and you are free to do so at your own time, pace and energy. Because your focus is on one book of the bible or a few books totaling 6 chapters, you will have gained much study, that many Christians wish they could achieve here on earth. Sadly, in some persecution areas, Christians do not even get time to read the entire bible!

4. Willing to work

The results of being an independent student is the freedom to work! Yes, you should focus on studies as an independent student, but because you have no strings attached, you can begin working on things that matter! You could begin working in the fields and planting sweet corn, potatoes and other garden produce that may be used on your own table or on the table of a needy group of people. You can find ways to do odd-jobs from painting to fixing fences to roofing and even building homes. It all depends on how you like to serve. Work atmosphere as a student should not be more than 10 hours a week, else studies are abandoned, and work becomes the focus. Because the student is not using an enrollment program for full-time status at a college, the debts are likely to be lower in the independent student. However, make sure that work-style debts are not accumulated, such as purchasing a business or supplies to make something. This creates burdens in the independent student. It is best to wait for major debts to be purchased, if needed at all in the individual who is 25 years or older, after more wisdom is established. Be wise in use of money and time and be dedicated to work in ways that will serve others in the future as well as your future family!

5. Willing to serve

All in all the bible is the book that teaches people how to serve others better! Without it, we are a distraction, an up rooter, a scorner and a terrible witness to the rest of the world. Without knowledge of cultures, tribes and tongues, we are at a loss in how to love the people better and how better to understand their pain. The results of a liberal arts bible college degree, is not in the selfish pride of knowledge. It is in the overcoming of self and willingness to serve others better out of the depth of our heart and the ability of Christ's strength within us. It is not to be used as a political force but as a divine force of eternal love. Colleges and seminaries may be willing to work with our process of gaining knowledge independently! Maybe you may actually work with a professor who can grant you your specific degree which is entitled in a book of the bible. It may not be qualified as accredited according to the world-system, but your specific college may actually work with your studies and grant you special credits. Maybe you can begin working in a specific field as they see your strength in study has shown you are more capable than ever in working with them in their company or business. Thus, these studies that you complete independently qualify you as more capable than ever to love, understand, improve and serve humanity! To the general world, a major in a book of the bible is seen as ineffective witness, but to humanity as a whole, such majors and students are needed more than ever. The depth that you choose to cherish and gain knowledge of Christ rather than gaining the whole world, gives you a soul and heart for the people in your community, country and world at large!

Resources

1. Samples

*****Possible Categories and Course Title Ideas******

Accounting

Introduction to Accounting: Terms, Practice, Moral Immoral Behaviors, Examples, Money Principles in Bible, Effectiveness of principles from [Obadiah]

Fundamentals of Accounting: Business Terms, Inventories, Assets, Practice Problems

Accounting For Decision Making:

Directed Study:

Intermediate Accounting:

Frugality Management:

Wealth Management:

Accounting for Government, Church or Non-Profit:

Manager Accounting:

Accessing Quality Accounting:

Taxation:

Minority Studies

African People

Asian People

Native-Indigenous People

Latino People

Middle Eastern People

Jewish People

Self-sustainable, Isolated Community European and Serbia People

Unique Literature and Historical Stories of ** People

Unique Language and Celebrations of ** People

Natural Living of ** People

Struggles in Modern World of ** People

Woman Victories and Sufferings of ** People

Slavery causes and Effects of ** People

Anthropology
Cultural Anthropology

Biological Anthropology

Household Management Anthropology

Art (expand into further topics and classes)

Athletic

Biology Nature

Chemistry

Classics

Communication

Computer Science

Dance

Economics

Education

English

Environmental Studies and Frugal Living

Language Specific (French, Spanish, Native American...)

History

Journalism

Classical Languages

Management

Mathematics

Music

Nursing

Philosophy

Physics

Political Science

Psychology

Religion

Science and Astronomy

Sociology and Work

Theater, Voice and Drama

Women, Womanhood vs. Feminism, Midwifery and Widowhood

***Fill in other topics you desire to study in your Liberal Arts education

-

*****Sample 4 Credit Class*****

4 credit class includes 16-17 weeks of materials

Blocks of time include 1 hour sessions 3 times a week or 1 and 1/2 hour sessions two times a week.

Book Materials Used: Mozart the Man and the Artist, as revealed in his own words by FRIEDRICH KERST (
Chopin: The man and his music by James Huneker (14 chapters), HAYDN By J. Cuthbe
Beethoven, the Man and the Artist, as Revealed in His Own Words by Beethoven by

Choose 5 musical pieces to study for each composer. Each musical piece will be studied each week.

Reports: Include studies from research outside of class literature given. Includes questions and ideas re

Quizes: Asks fact information about literature in class, information about musical pieces from each comp
memorization of bible and questions about comparison between composer to bibli

Memorization: Bible verses, Statements from literature, musical pieces

Session Number	Activity	Biblical Focus	Quiz/Repc
Session 1	Read Introduction and Chapter	Song 1 and Law	Report
Session 2	Read Chapter 2 from Mozart	Song 2 and Old Testament	Quiz
Session 3	Read Chapter 3 from Mozart	Song 3 and Psalms/Proverbs	Memoriza
Session 4	Read Chapter 4 from Mozart	Song 4 and Gospel	Report
Session 5	Read Chapter 5 from Mozart	Song 5 and New Testament	Quiz
Session 6	Read Chapter 6 from Mozart	Song 6 and Law	Memoriza
Session 7	Read Chapter 7 from Mozart	Song 7 and Old Testament	Report
Session 8	Read Chapter 8 from Mozart	Song 8 and Psalms/Proverbs	Quiz
Session 9	Read Chapter 9 from Mozart	Song 1 and Gospel	Memoriza
Session 10	Read Chapter 10 from Mozart	Song 2 and New Testament	Report
Session 11	Read Chapter 11 from Mozart	Song 3 and Law	Quiz
Session 12	Read Chapter 12 from Mozart	Song 4 and Old Testament	Memoriza
Session 13	Read Chapter 13 from Mozart	Song 5 and Psalms/Proverbs	Report
Session 14	Read Chapter 14 from Mozart	Song 6 and Gospel	Quiz
Session 15	Read Chapter 15 from Mozart	Song 7 and New Testament	Memoriza
Session 16	Read Chapter 16- 17 to end fro	Song 8 and Law	Report
Session 17	Mini Mozart Test and Begin Rea	Song 1 and Old Testament	Quiz
Session 18	Read Chapter 1-2 from Beethov	Song 2 and Psalms/Proverbs	Memoriza
Session 19	Read Chapter 3 from Beethove	Song 3 and Gospel	Report
Session 20	Read Chapter 4 from Beethove	Song 4 and New Testament	Quiz
Session 21	Read Chapter 5 from Beethove	Song 5 and Law	Memoriza
Session 22	Read Chapter 6 from Beethove	Song 6 and Old Testament	Report
Session 23	Read Chapter 7 from Beethove	Song 7 and Psalms/Proverbs	Quiz
Session 24	Read Chapter 8 from Beethove	Song 8 and Gospel	Memoriza
Session 25	Mid-Semester TEST	Mid-Semester TEST	Semester
Session 26	Read Chapter 9 from Beethove	Song 1 and New Testament	Report
Session 27	Read Chapter 10 from Beethov	Song 2 and Law	Quiz

*****Sample Schedule*****

Weekly Schedule for a Student. The student believes in celebrating a weekly Sabbath (same can apply to anyother worship time)

Time	1	2	3	4	5	6	7
8:00	C: Biblical Archeology	S: Musical Repretoire	C: Biblical Archeology	S: Musical Repretoire	C: Biblical Archeology	S: Musical Repretoire	
9:00	S: Biblical Archeology	C: Musical Repretoire	S: Biblical Archeology	C: Musical Repretoire	S: Biblical Archeology	SS-Open	
10:00	C: Natural Bio. Lab	C(1/2): Musical Repretoire	C: Natural Bio. Lab	C(1/2): Musical Repretoire	C: Natural Bio. Lab	SS-Open	
11:00	Meal	Meal	Meal	Meal	Meal	Meal	
12:00	S: Natural Biology	C: Natural Biology	S: Natural Biology	C: Natural Biology	S: Natural Biology	C: Natural Biology	
1:00	SS-Open	C: Physical Fitness	SS-Open	C: Physical Fitness	SS-Open	Extra Curr.: Volunteer	
2:00	Extra Curr.: Music	SS-Open	Extra Curr.: Music	C: Physical Health	SS-Open	SS-Open	
3:00	S: Phys. Fitness/Health	S: Phys. Fitness/Health	S: Phys. Fitness/Health	C: Physical Health	S: Phys. Fitness/Health	S: Phys. Fitness/Health	
4:00	Extra Curr.: Visit Elderly	SS-Open	Extra Curr.: Visit Elderly	SS-Open	Extra Curr.: Visit Elderly	Rest At Sunset	
5:00	SS-Open	SS-Open	SS-Open	SS-Open	SS-Open		
6:00	Meal	Meal	Meal	Meal	Meal		
7:00	SS-Open	SS-Open	SS-Open	SS-Open	Meal		
8:00	SS-Open	SS-Open	Evening Group Extra.	SS-Open			
9:00	SS-Open	SS-Open	SS-Open	SS-Open			
10:00			Prep at sunset				

Classes: Biblical Archeology and Discussions from book of Job (4 credit), Musical Repretoire of 16th century with comparisons to Book of 2 Chronicles an Job (4 credit), Natural Biology in coordination with book of Job (4 credit), Physical Fitness with memorizations from Phillipians and Job (2 credit), Physical Health with Discussions from Job (2 Credit;

The Student is Major is in the Book of Job.

Major in the Book of [Obadiah]

An example of a major in the book of [Obadiah]

I know that sounds like a funny and unimportant major in this world, but think about it, we humans are created to worship God and nothing else. Everything else fails. Terrorists get a hold of certain realms of knowledge and use it against humanity. Anyone living in this century knows this to be true.

So what is the solution????

A degree in the book of _____

Year One:
Teaching [Obadiah] to children 5 and under. 4 credits
Writing from [Obadiah]. 4 Credits
Study of [Obadiah] in the modern world. 4 Credits
Cultural Origination of [Obadiah]. 4 Credits

Year Two:
Correlation of [Obadiah] to [Proverbs] in Logical Algorithm. 4 Credits
Applying [Obadiah] to Variant Writings. 4 Credits
[Obadiah] use in Natural One Spouse Marriage. 4 Credits
Observational [Obadiah] aspects to creation study . 4 Credits

Year Three:
Mathematical Application and Studies of [Obadiah]. 4 Credits
Ethical applications of [Obadiah]. 4 Credits
Native and Tribal studies of [Obadiah]. 4 Credits
Dictionary and Library Science with [Obadiah]. 4 Credits

Year Four:
Application of [Obadiah] to modern/current technology. 4 Credits
Memorization and Performance of [Obadiah]. 4 Credits
Sustainable life and community with principles from [Obadiah] 4 Credits
Language and Alternate and Origins of [Obadiah] 4 Credits

Additional Studies Can include the following (four per year are selected):
Producing book of [Obadiah] to art. 3 Credits
Producing book of [Obadiah] to Multimedia. 3 Credits

Interrelation of book of [Obadiah] to Music. 3 Credits
Study and Practice in Sports to book of [Obadiah]. 4 Credits
Celestial and Microorganism Study of Book of [Obadiah]. 4 Credits
Creative Writing with book of [Obadiah] 4 credits
Engaging [Obadiah] to household management. 4 Credits
Application of multigenerational church to book of [Obadiah] 4 Credits
Study of word and Communication arrangements and effects by book of [Obadiah] 4 Credits
Teaching book of [Obadiah] to age 6-12. 4 Credits
Training teenager, the new Christian and the faulty Christian in the book of [Obadiah] 4 Credits
Creating Learning Games in book of [Obadiah] 4 Credits
Investigation of Medicine and Ethical Principals according to the book of [Obadiah] 4 Credits

A Typical 4 Credit Class would consist of:
25 pages per day of reading material in relation to the topic
10 point quizzes each week
Memorization tests of 100 words each week
2 Exams
1-5 page paper per week
20 page final paper
Publish one book each year according to four of the variant subjects
Character improvement checklist per each subject studied

Other Subject Matters that may be perfected according to the book of [Obadiah]
-Carpentry
-Painting
-Calligraphy
-Arts
-Science Subjects
-Mathematics
-Accounting
-Social Applications and Readings including general Statistical Survey
-Psychology Applications and Readings
-Creative Literature
-Sport and Physical
-Language Arts
-Life and Wild Life Skills
-Cooking
-Maternity and Death Subjects
-Healthcare Subjects
-Crafts
-Language Studies in repetition conversation and translation of scripture

-Martyrs and Sufferings of yesterday and Today
-Women and speaking kindly in home and towards male authority
-Unhindered Living

Acceptance:
-Serving Actively in good standing within the community or current living arrangements
-Live with parents while under study and apprenticeship
-Have taken a full conservative biblical study resource
-Understand biblical calendar, Fibonacci formula and such in relation to creation study as well as arrangement of Passover and musical applications in relation to nature
-Practice positive biblical reading pattern on regular basis.
-Provide a daily journal and reflection from scripture
-Signed arrangement to not Sell the "super-knowledge" of God's word but rather to work in a simple job. In other words making a big profit off of knowledge of God's truth.
-Basic Accumulation of Knowledge to succeed in ACT, SAT and such knowledge tests.

Students:
-Completely independent study
-Submit Syllabus for daily work
-Submit daily assignments and quizzes
-All work is returned each month to help write book each year.
-Other Subject Matter Syllabus Submitted
-Daily assignments for "other" study also submitted and worked to perfection.

There is another resource out there that also assists parents and others interested in a fuller study of biblical knowledge, it is www.sonlighteducation.com

****Sample Test, Sample Quiz, Sample Paper Topics****

Test: Questions – 20 Questions, Write in Answers – 5, Essay Response – 2, Time Allowed 50 minutes.

Test Title: Verbal Reasoning in English and in Biblical Themes from Numbers

1.   Some children are sitting in three rows all facing North such that A is in the middle row. P is just to the right of A but in the same row. Q is just behind of P while R is in the North of A. In which direction of R is Q?

A.   South

B.   South-West

C.   North-East

D.   South-East

2. In the scripture it indicates in Num. 3:29 "The families of the sons of Kohath shall pitch on the side of the tabernacle southward." According to this chapter how many were numbered among the family of Merari that encamped southward? (look up information)

A.   6,200

B.   4,500

C.   information not available

D.   3,200

3. If P + Q means P is the brother of Q; P x Q means P is the father of Q and P - Q means P is the sister of Q, which of the following relations shows that I is the niece of K?

A.   K + Y + Z - I

B.   K + Y x I - Z

C.   Z - I x Y + K

D.   K x Y + I - Z

4. Numbers 3:32 And Eleazar the son of Aaron the priest shall be chief over the chief of the Levites, and have the oversight of them that keep the charge of the sanctuary.

33 Of Merari was the family of the Mahlites, and the family of the Mushites: these are the families of Merari.

34 And those that were numbered of them, according to the number of all the males, from a month old and upward, were six thousand and two hundred.

35 And the chief of the house of the father of the families of Merari was Zuriel the son of Abihail: these shall pitch on the side of the tabernacle northward.

36 And under the custody and charge of the sons of Merari shall be the boards of the tabernacle, and the bars thereof, and the pillars thereof, and the sockets thereof, and all the vessels thereof, and all that serveth thereto,

From the passage given, from what tribe did Zuriel come from?

A.   Kohathites

B.   Ephraim

C.   Levites

D.   Judah

172

....

Write in answers:

1. Describe how 'responsibility' was essential in the first three chapters of the book of Numbers. Explain why responsibility cannot coexist with irresponsibility according to the chapters:_____

2. The 'east side' of the tabernacle contained which tribe. What reason did God possibly place this tribe on the East side according to the first three chapters in the book of Numbers and according to previous information you gather?

......

Essay:

What method would you use to describe relationship between God, Moses, Tribe, Congregations, Priests and Captain? How were the people in the tribes arranged according to biblical definitions? What causes the males to be numbered from one month old and upward? What character behavior did the people have towards following the commands?

Quiz: Questions – 15 Questions, Memorization Questions – 5, Time Allowed: 20 minutes

Quiz Title: Arguments in Philosophy and in Psalms 1-5

1. The word "philosophy" derives from: Language _____ Meaning_____

2. A philosophical argument is a form of verbal disagreement.

A. TRUE

B. FALSE

3. The ungodly are like _____ and _____ according to Psalm 1.

4. Define counsel. Indicate how definition is derived.:

.....

Memorization:

1. Psalm 1

2. Definitions of Monists, Pluralists, Rationalists, Empiricists

Paper Topics:

American Colonization and Considerations in the 1st and 2nd Corinthians.

 For class: Artistic English Writings in Accordance to the Corinthians

A new country is born!

Write a theme story about events that happened in the Boston Tea Party. Spin the event to show your favor or disfavor for this event. Consider how Corinthians themes and topics would shape this event. One could describe interesting things that happened like the revolutionaries dressing up as Native Americans.

Paper Length: 1-2 pages double spaced

Evaluations: Grammar, Spelling, Content, Life, Biblical Relationship, Historical Accuracy

2. Book lists

Make a variety of book lists to keep your mind and heart knowledge driven. Assume you will read one or more books per week. Here are some ideas for creating lists:

-General Knowledge

-Home and Family

-Survival

-Christian literature

-Culture

-College Enhancement

-STEM

-Music, Arts

Here is a sample book list that allows a person to study a variety of subjects when time is limited to study things deeply.

1 Pilgrim Church by E.H. Broadbent   -FREE- www.truthforfree.com

2 Pilgrim's Progress John Bunyan   -FREE- www.gutenberg.org

3 Daniel Deronda by George Eliot   -FREE- www.gutenberg.org

4 Alice's Adventures in Wonderland   -FREE- Amazon kindle version

5 Ask Jackie Gardening by Jackie Clay-Atkinson   -FREE- Amazon kindle version at moment

6 E-books by Candy Brauer   -FREE- www.joyfulchristianhomemaking.com

7 Covering   -FREE-
www.searchthescriptures.com

8 Wives and Daughters by Elizabeth Cleghom Gaskell -FREE- Amazon Kindle

9 Talks to Farmers   -FREE- www.gutenberg.org

10 50 Things Every young Lady Should Know -16.99-
www.booksonthepath.com

11 Mother: A Story by Kathleen T. Norris-FREE- www.gutenberg.org

12 Anna Karenina by Leo Tolstoy   -FREE- Amazon Kindle

13 Bleak House by Charles Dickens   -FREE- Amazon Kindle

14 Abigail Adams and Her Times by Laura EH Richards -FREE-
www.gutengerg.org

15 Who Are the Clergy by David Yeubanks   -FREE-
www.truthforfree.com

16 So Much More by Anna Sofia Botkin -17.99-
www.booksonthepath.com

17 Sisters by Kathleen Thompson Norris -FREE- www.gutenberg.org

18 Anthem by Ayn Rand   -FREE- Amazon Kindle

19 Does God hold the Christian accountable to keep the Saturday
Sabbath? -FREE- www.searchthescriptures.com

20 Elsie Dinsmore by Martha Finley   -FREE- Amazon Kindle

21 Should the veiling of Christian women be practiced all of the time? -
FREE- www.searchthescriptures.com

22 How to Raise a Gentleman by Kay West   -16.99-
www.booksonthepath.com

23 An Alabaster Box by Mary Eleanor Wilkins -FREE-
www.gutenberg.org

24 Gleanings Among the Sheaves   -FREE-
www.gutenberg.org

25 Natural Medicine For children by Julian Scott PhD   Home Library

26 Dressing for the glory of God   -FREE-
www.searchthescriptures.com

27 Complete Guide to Needlework   by Reader's Digest   Home
collection

28 Gleanings Among the Sheaves   -FREE- www.grace-e-
books.com

29 Kate's Ordeal by Emma Leslie   -FREE-
www.gutenberg.org

30 THE BEAUTIFUL AND DAMNED BY F. SCOTT FITZGERALD -FREE-
Amazon Kindle

31 The Way of a Man with a Maid by Robin Phillips   -FREE-
www.truthforfree.com

32 The Cabin on the Prairie by CH Pearson-FREE- Amazon Kindle

33 50 years in the Church of Rome -FREE- www.archive.org

34 Mathew Henry's Concise Commentary on the Bible -FREE-
www.grace-ebooks.com

35 Hints on Child Training by H Clay Thumbull   -7.99-
www.booksonthepath.com

36 Nutrition and Physical Degeneration -FREE-
gutenberg.net.au/ebooks02/0200251h.html

37 Did the apostles of Christ teach and practice legalism -FREE-
www.searchthescriptures.com

38 A Manual of Homemaking by Rensselaer, Rose, Canon - FREE-
www.archive.org

39 Atlantic Narratives: Modern Short Stories;-FREE- www.gutenberg.org

40 Dictionary--Read Webster's Dictionary and select words unknown

41 Two Indian Children of Long Ago by Frances Lillian Taylor -FREE-
www.homeschoolfreebie.wholesomechildhood.com

42 The Merchant Maiden: Earning an Income Without Compromising
Convictions by Crystal Paine -FREE-
www.homeschoolfreebie.wholesomechildhood.com

43 Twenty-Six Hours a Day by Mary Blake -FREE- www.archive.org

44 The apostles doctrine on the place of faith for Christian women -
FREE- www.searchthescriptures.com

45 The Heart Remembers by June Masters Bacher -home library-

46 Breaking the Jewish Code by Perry Stone -home library-

47 ACT Assessment Success (I'd go for GRE but this'll do for intellectual
benefit) -home library-

48 The Christian's Secret of a Happy Life by Hannah Whitall Smith -FREE-
www.archive.org

49 Just Starting by Renee Ellison -small price, e-book-
www.homeschoolhowtos.com

50 Mastering Your Bernina -FREE- from bernina website

51 The cure of Imperfect Sight by Treatment without Glasses -FREE- www.archeive.org

52 The Best of Crystal's Blog by Crystal Paine -small price e-book- not sure if still available

53 (additional) Chucking College http://www.chuckingcollege.com/Home.html by Melanie Ellison

54 (additional) Free e-books from homeschool howtos https://homeschoolhowtos.com/store/list/category/free_e_books

3. I'm busy but I can read books

101 Ways to Read and Use KJV Bible

[joy] means another word can replace the word like [praise], [gold] etc.
You may also use other literature with these activities too.

1. Cross Stitch a picture from a verse or word.
2. Write 25 verses about [joy].
3. Memorize above activity [2]
4. Make a crossword with a [25] word string.
5. Make a word find with a [25] word string.
6. Develop a children's book from a 10 verse passage.
7. Write an essay about a hot topic, include words from 10 verse passage.
8. Study a specific topic like [servants].
9. Sew a quilt and add patches with +bible verse or pictures.
10. Write a comic from 10 verses or words randomly selected. I will continue with the rest later.

11. Study the Biblical Calendar and Learn When Noah Landed the Ark (yes it is different than January, February Calendar)
12. Locate all the different Herbs mentioned in the bible and identify their positive and negative health effects.
13. Create a 25 point quiz about one chapter in the bible.
14. Make thank-you cards with bible verses.
15. Write a short story and include words and verses from one chapter of the bible.
16. Make a prayer list of 50 + people that you know personally, face to face and distantly through internet interactions. Pick verses to base a prayer off of. Try writing 50 prayers. Pray daily.
17. Make a garden ornament out of a randomly selected verse and/or word.
18. Read a whole chapter in Hebrew or Greek or another language.
19. Get friends and play Pictionary off of the various words found in a 10 verse portion.
20. Make animal flashcards of the animals in the bible.

21. Play story line game. Take a portion or verse and add silly words. "Great Ice Cream Cones are thy...." Ask friend to id. silly word
22. Make screen print t-shirt out of randomly selected KJV verse.
23. Create a skit out of random 10 verse portion. Make funny! Make Sad!

24. Quote it backwards. See how far you can quote 10 verse portion backwards.

25. Make a puzzle out of 220+ verses.

26. Randomly select 10 verses. See how well you can fill in blank with missing words.

27. Create a hopscotch game of fancy design with 10 verse portion.

28. Do an old-Fashioned radio show with 10 verse portion. Sound Effects etc.

29. Write a nice note to a friend on social network site using words from 1 verse.

30. Define All words in a 10 verse portion. Write them down and use in essay or book.

31. Make music out of a couple verses.

32. Play Balderdash. Use selected chapters or verses. Define words from the passages.

33. Study Genesis 10. Determine your origin.

34. Select 10 verse portion. See how much you can write without looking and without error.

35. Play scramble. See how fast you can make crossword out of the words from 10 verses at a set time.

36. Identify map locations in the bible today and in history.

37. Make a small movie out of randomly selected 10 verse portion.

38. Write a special letter to your spouse or friend using all words from 10 verse portion.

39. Verse Guess. Location? What verse says?

40. Write a poem using all words from a verse.

41. Meditate on 10 verses a week. Random or Subject

42. I.D. all verbs that Christ spoke. Write down verses that accompany.

43. Bad Song in your head? Use tune but replace with words from KJV psalms.

44. Bad thought in mind? Use words, story from KJV to replace and come up with a new thought.

45. Temptation? (Smoking, drinking, depression, sexual impurity etc). Select 10 verses. Make a card with the verses and meditate on the verses

46. Play [hangman] with various words. Battleship, categories, spelling etc.

47. ID parts of speech. In a verse.

48. Read 5 psalms per day within 30 days. (Try 3 years no fail!)

49. Read Proverb chapter per day according to the day of the month. ie. 2nd day of month read proverbs 2. (Try 3 years no fail!)

50. Study book of [proverbs]. Study all the information you can from individual verses. Use other sources to id. specifics.

51. Make birthday cards with verses.
52. Make child's toy, game puzzle from a [word, verse, story]
53. Have a child copy verses in cursive. 1 a day.
54. Study foods mentioned in the bible. Make a 2 week menu plan from the foods.
55. Design website, blog, computer program using a verse, chapter or story from the bible.
56. Design a simple business plan from a short passage.
57. Write a letter to a politician using 10 words from a passage.
58. Create a simple lesson for [young child, youth, adult] from randomly selected chapter.
59. Do a puppet show of randomly selected passage.
60. Do sign language of entire verse or passage.

A * indicates methods to educate and teach. Helpful in accomplishing bachelor level of education.
61. Look at classical Artwork of selected word, verse or passage
62. Help pre-reader read 10 words in passage
63. Read a bible passage to a widow.
64. Draw an unusual drawing from a [verse, passage] 2 Cor 7:10 try memory style drawing
65. Have a pre-reader identify dolch sight words from passage.
66. Have a child draw a picture from verse/passage.
67. See a living thing? See if its mentioned in the bible.
68. *Narrate a passage from the bible in own words
69. *Draw Stick Figures of passage/verse.
70. *Skill mentioned in the bible? Splinter into small parts and master the skill

71. *Skill mentioned in the bible? Conquer in short spurts Task-Chore-Task-Chore (variety in month etc)
72. *Skill mentioned in the bible? Specific task same time over and over.
73. *Schedule Active vs. Passive Activity. Sing bible verse, do something else. Write bible verse, exercise etc.
74. *Teach/ Learn during high times - 8 P.M./After meal etc. Incorporate 1 verse or passage.
75. *Memory Moments. In line, while waiting for appointment. Incorporate what you are memorizing with bible verses.
76. *Teach for whole body instruction. in bible passage ID sight, hear, smell etc.
77. *Use analogy or object when possible. ie. use two boards glued together as two become one etc.
78. *Drive into inner speech. Say whisper, think random 10 [word, verse,

passage]
79. *Sink an emotional hook. ie. Read about 10 plagues then study nature of frogs from [5] sources and give quiz.
80. *Get another angle from [word, verse, passage] using 68 - 79 above.

81. *Use Place-mat Grounding. (Timeline, World map, Big Lists) Use bible verse, word passage to id.
82. *Train Keen Details. Use [word, verse, passage] and (Draw details, parts, definitions etc)
83. *Don't Delegate too soon. (Do [patience/joy] 25 x's correctly) ID. other positive character words in bible and do correct with different activities.
84. *Practice critical thinking skills with various hot topic mentioned in Bible.
85. *Busy Children are Happy Children. Schedule 10 bible based activities for young children.
86. *Teach mastery not just plow through. Id. a bible verse, activity etc. and master it.
87. Listen to a story or sermon. ID words or verses that are also mentioned in bible.
88. Pick a (word, verse, phrase) at random. Create a gift for someone else. (family, disabled etc)
89. Practice forgiveness. Write a list of family, friends, neighbors, community who hurt you. In list columns write name, what they did, verse to overcome, and write what you would say as forgiveness. Perhaps tell the person personally.
90. Practice [verb Christ spoke, other verb] write people's names, verse to help, plan to accomplish in column form.

91. Improve vision with others. Create positive psychology with a random verse. Write down "I will be patient with John." Write 5 statements and say 3 times each day for one week.
92. Meditate on 5-10 verses while jogging, exercising, lifting weights etc.
93. Improve work ethic. Randomly select [word, verse, passage]. Envision yourself and say to yourself you will improve according to verse. Write down steps as necessary.
94. Create a to-do-list, project based off of bible [word, verse, passage].
95. Study why a randomly selected [word, verse, passage] is in the bible.
96. See an inanimate or other object [gold, coins, mosquito etc]. Identify where this thing fits in creation story. Study science behind its behavior.
97. Read a book, poem, subject on [word, verse, passage] found in bible. Study and create tests.
98. Ugly media story? ID. what one or more of the 10 commandments was broken in the life of that character. Try God's law too!
99. Improve English skills using KJV bible when writing anything.

100. Create social science experiment comparing biblical [passage, verse, word] verses current cultural practice.

101. Create 101 MORE bible based activities based off of bible itself, other sources, creative skills etc. here's a few more. ********>>>>>
102. Create a home church service. Let words in red stand for the pastor or preacher, read a chapter of psalms , 1 random old testament and one random new testament chapter. Include old hymns, prayers and such.
103. Study psalm 119. For each verse identify what you will do vs. what God will do...... Write it down.
If you have mastered these, tell others. And you will receive blessing!
****Make as many copies as you would like and pass these out to strangers, family n' friends!

Highlight Your Bible Study Method

*Buy a set of colorful highlighters and colored pencils. Highlight according to topic.
YELLOW = salvation, Jesus is the only way
PINK = promises, prophecy, special gifts / rewards
GREEN = wisdom, prosperity, special command, law
BLUE = anti-cult, discernment, certain distinctions
ORANGE = Caution, Warning
BROWN = verbal emotions of God, Behaviors of a Godly person
PINK UNDERLINE = Woman, wife, mother, widow duties...
GREEN UNDERLINE = Children, child training....
BLUE UNDERLINE = Men, Husband, Father duties.....
Double UNDERLINE = Younger, servant, under authority duties
Dash UNDERLINE = Older, Master, Elder, in authority duties

Bondages

*When a person follows Christ through daily bible study, prayer, sharing gospel with others and mediation on scripture, these bondages can and will PERMANENTLY get eliminated.
*Avoiding social situations, watching movies or reading books that engross in these things can help overcome these bondages

*Daily ask yourself if you are having addictions or problems in any of these areas. In three years time of walking with Christ, most of these issues should not be a problem.

Gambling addictions
Sexual impurity (homosexuality, fornication, divorce and remarriage, co-habitation etc.)
pornography addictions
alcoholism
depression
mental-illness
confusions and lies from society
anger
eating disorders
guilt
failure

*Note: any who come to Christ and trust him may get persecuted from authorities, family or others.... keep fighting the good fight of faith anyway!

Notebook Study Method

*Write out each of these topics on the top of a page in a notebook. Write verses that coordinate and discuss these topics

Assurance and Promises
Battling Principalities and Powers of Darkness
Barean (study the scripture)
Blessings from heaven
Called and Chosen
Character Building
Christ Yeshua Savior
Christian Duty
Confession
Death
Examples from Past
Faith
Feasts
Forgiveness
Glories of Heaven
Health
Hope
Humility and Meekness
Hunger and Thirst for Truth
Joy
Kindness and Goodness
Love
Obedience
Patience
Peacemakers
Persecuted for Righteousness
Power and equipping
Praise and Worship
Prayer
Prophesies fulfilled
Prophesies yet Future
Rebuke and Warning
Response to Slander and Divisiveness
Revealer of the Heart
Self Control
Selfless Love
Sickness
Sorrow
Time of now and Future
Truth in Scripture
Unrighteous Results
Victorious Living

Truthfulness
Alertness
Self-Thoroughness
Discretion
Punctuality
Humility
Compassion
Boldness
Flexibility
Dependability
Love
Tolerance
Decisiveness
Gentleness
Forgiveness
Availability
Security
Creativity
Cautiousness
Determination
Deference
Persuasiveness
Endurance
Patience
Enthusiasm
Gratefulness
Loyalty
Meekness

Parashah Style Weekly Readings	Torah Law	Prophets and Books	Gospel	New Testament
1	Gen 1:1-6:8	Joshua 1-11	Matt 1-2	Acts 1-3
2	Gen 6:9-11:32	Joshua 12-22	Matt 3-4	Acts 4-6
3	Gen 12:1-17:27	Josh 23-Jud 9	Matt 5-6	Acts 7-9
4	Gen 18:1-22:24	Judges 10-21	Matt 7-8	Acts 10-12
5	Gen 23:1-25:18	Ruth-1 Sam 7	Matt 9-10	Acts 13-15
6	Gen 25:19-28:9	1 Sam 8-19	Matt 11-12	Acts 16-18
7	Gen 28:10-32:3	1 Sam 20-31	Matt 13-14	Acts 19-21
8	Gen 32:4-36:43	2 Sam 1-11	Matt 15-16	Acts 22-24
9	Gen 37:1-40:23	2 Sam 12-23	Matt 17-18	Acts 25-27
10	Gen 41:1-44 -:17	2 Sam 24-1 K 10	Matt 19-20	Acts 28-Rom 2
11	Gen 44:18-47:27	1 K 11-22	Matt 21-22	Rom 3-5
12	Gen 47:28-50:26	2 K 1-11	Matt 23-24	Rom 6-8
13	Ex 1:1-6:1	2 K 12-23	Matt 25-26	Rom 9-11
14	Ex 6:2-9:35	2 K 24-1 Chr 9	Matt 27-28	Rom 12-14
15	Ex 10:1-13:16	1 Chr 10-21	Mark 1-2	Rom 15-1 Cor 1
16	Ex 13:17-17:16	1 Chr 22-2 Chr 4	Mark 3-4	1 Cor 2-4
17	Ex 18:1-20:23	2 Chr 5-16	Mark 5-6	1 Cor 5-7
18	Ex 21:1-24:18	2 Chr 17-28	Mark 7-8	1 Cor 8-10
19	Ex 25:1-27:19	2 Chr 29-Ezr 4	Mark 9-10	1 Cor 11-13
20	Ex 27:20-30:10	Ezr 5-Neh 6	Mark 11-12	1 Cor 14-16
21	Ex 30:11-34:35	Neh 7-Esth 5	Mark 13-14	2 Cor 1-3
22	Ex 35:1-38:20	Esth 6-Job 7	Mark 15-16	2 Cor 4-6
23	Ex 38:21-40:38	Job 8-Job 20	Luke 1-2	2 Cor 7-9
24	Lev 1:1-5:26	Job 21-32	Luke 3-4	2 Cor 10-12
25	Lev 6:1-8:36	Job 33-Ecc 2 *no Ps Pr	Luke 5-6	2 Cor 13-Gal 2
26	Lev 9:1-11:47	Ecc 3-S Song 2	Luke 7-8	Gal 3-5
27	Lev 12:1-13:59	S Song 3 - Is 4	Luke 9-10	Gal 6-Eph 2
28	Lev 14:1-15:33	Is 5-16	Luke 11-12	Eph 3-5
29	Lev 16:1-18:30	Is 17-28	Luke 13-14	Eph 6-Phil 2
30	Lev 19:1-20:27	Is 29-40	Luke 15-16	Phil3- Col 2
31	Lev 21:1-24:23	Is 41-52	Luke 17-18	Col 3-1 Thes 1
32	Lev 25:1-26:2	Is 53-64	Luke 19-20	1 Thes 2-4
33	Lev 26:3-27:34	Is 65-Jer 9	Luke 21-22	1 Thes 5 - 2 Thes 2
34	Num 1:1-4:20	Jer 10-21	Luke 23-24	2 Thes 3-1 Tim2
35	Num 4:21-7:89	Jer 22-33	John 1-2	1 Tim 3-5
36	Num 8:1-12:16	Jer 34-45	John 3-4	1 Tim 6-2 Tim 2
37	Num 13:1-15:41	Jer 46-Lamen	John 5-6	2 Tim 3-Titus 1
38	Num 16:1-18:32	Ez 1-11	John 7-8	Titus 2-3
39	Num 19:1-22:1	Ez 12-23	John 9-10	Phil -Heb 2
40	Num 22:2-25:9	Ez 24-35	John 11-12	Heb 3-5
41	Num 25:10-30:1	Ez 36-47	John 13-14	Heb 6-8
42	Num 30:2-32:42	Ez 48-Dan 10	John 15-16	Heb 9-11
43	Num 33:1-36:13	Dan 11-Hos 9	John 17-18	Heb 12-James 1
44	Deut 1:1-3:22	Hos 10-Amos 3	John 19-20	James 2-4
45	Deut 3:23-7:11	Amos 4-Jonah	John 21	James 5-1 Pet 2
46	Deut 7:12-11:25	Micah-Hab 1	Rand 1-14	1 Pet 3-5
47	Deut 11:26-16:17	Hab 2-Haggai	Rand 1-14	2 Peter
48	Deut 16:18-21:9	Zechariah 1-11	Rand 15-22	1 John 1-3
49	Deut 21:10-25:19	Zech 12-Malachi	Rand 15-22	1 John 4-2 John
50	Deut 26:1-29:8	Random Selection	Rand 23-34	3 John, Jude, Rev 1-2
51	Deut 29:9-30:20	Random Selection	Rand 23-34	Rev 3-7
52	Deut 31:1-31:30	Random Selection	Rand 35-45	Rev 8-12
53	Deut 32:1-52	Random Selection	Rand 35-45	Rev 13-17
54	Deut 33:1-34:12	Random Selection	Random S	Rev 18-22

How to Use: *Start the Reading Pattern when Full-Moon is below Virgo immediately after Spring Equinox. Allign to Astronomical Signs in the heavens......
*Use Monthly Pattern of 30 Days and additional day each season (Qumran Calendar method)
*Complete each reading on Sabbath and throughout week
*Read Proverbs and Psalms according to day of month. 5 Psalms on 1st day of month (1, 31, 61, 91, 121) Prov 1. 2nd day of month (2, 32, 62, 92, 122). Continue pattern.

**** Use a computer generated randomizer to select weekly readings OR follow through readings in order during entire year. 2 Additional weeks are for holy

Psalms and Proverbs Readings

How to determine what to read each day:

Determine day of the month. Read psalms according to the pattern.

1. 1, 31, 61, 91, 121
2. 2, 32, 62, 92, 122
3. 3, 33, 63, 93, 123
4. 4, 34, 64, 94, 124
5. 5, 35, 65, 95, 125
6. 6, 36, 66, 96, 126
7. 7, 37, 67, 97, 127
8. 8, 38, 68, 98, 128
9. 9, 39, 69, 99, 129
10. 10, 40, 70, 100, 130
1*. 1*, 4*, 7*, 10*, 13*
2*. 2*, 5*, 8*, 11*, 14*
30. 30, 60, 90, 120, 150

*= insert last number in the date given ie. Day 24 of the month would use
2*, 5*, 8*, 11*, 14* to convert to 24, 54, 84,114,144 Psalms readings

Select the Proverb according to the day of the month except 31 for each
month with 30 days or less. Add the additional proverbs chapters.

4. Qumran Calendar

Abib 1 — Moon Rise Time: ___ Moon Location

1	2 PM	3	4
5	6	7	8	9	10	11
12	13	14	15	16	17	18
19	20	21	22	23	24	25
26	27	28	29	30		

4 — Moon Rise Time: ___ Moon Location

1	2	3	4
5	6	7	8	9	10	11
12	13	14	15	16	17	18
19	20	21	22	23	24	25
26	27	28 PM	29	30		

7 — Moon Rise Time: ___ Moon Location

1	2	3	4
5	6	7	8	9	10	11
12	13	14	15	16	17	18
19	20	21	22	23	24	25 PM
26	27	28	29	30		

10 — Moon Rise Time: ___ Moon Location

1	2	3	4
5	6	7	8	9	10	11
12	13	14	15	16	17	18
19	20	21	22	23 PM	24	25
26	27	28	29	30		

2 — Moon Rise Time: ___ Moon Location

1	2
3	4	5	6	7	8	9
10	11	12	13	14	15	16
17	18	19	20	21	22	23
24	25	26	27	28	29	30 PM

5 — Moon Rise Time: ___ Moon Location

1	2
3	4	5	6	7	8	9
10	11	12	13	14	15	16
17	18	19	20	21	22	23
24	25	26	27 PM	28	29	30

8 — Moon Rise Time: ___ Moon Location

1	2
3	4	5	6	7	8	9
10	11	12	13	14	15	16
17	18	19	20	21	22	23
24	25 PM	26	27	28	29	30

11 — Moon Rise Time: ___ Moon Location

1	2
3	4	5	6	7	8	9
10	11	12	13	14	15	16
17	18	19	20	21	22	23
24	25	26	27	28	29	30

3 — Moon Rise Time: ___ Moon Location

1	2	3	4	5	6	7
8	9	10	11	12	13	14
15	16	17	18	19	20	21
22	23	24	25	26	27	28
29 PM	30	SS				

6 — Moon Rise Time: ___ Moon Location

1	2	3	4	5	6	7
8	9	10	11	12	13	14
15	16	17	18	19	20	21
22	23	24	25	26	27 PM	28
29	30	AE				

9 — Moon Rise Time: ___ Moon Location

1	2	3	4	5	6	7
8	9	10	11	12	13	14
15	16	17	18	19	20	21
22	23	24 PM	25	26	27	28
29	30	WS				

12 — Moon Rise Time: ___ Moon Location

1	2	3	4	5	6	7
8	9	10	11	12	13	14
15	16	17	18	19	20	21
22 PM	23	24	25	26	27	28
29	30	SE				

Lunar Cycle 1
Hebrew Calendar Year ___
Qumran Calendar Rotation Number ___

Abib 1

			1≈	2	3	4
5	6	7≈	8	9	10≈	11
12≈	13≈ FM	14≈	15≈	16≈	17	18
19	20	21≈	22	23	24≈	25
26≈	27	28	29	30		

4

			1	2	3	4≈
5	6	7	8	9≈	10	11
12	13	14	15	16	17	18 FM
19	20	21	22	23	24	25
26	27	28	29	30		

7

			1≈	2	3	4
5	6	7	8	9	10≈	11
12	13	14	15≈ FM	16	17≈	18
19	20	21≈	22≈	23≈	24	25
26	27	28	29	30		

10

			1≈	2	3	4
5≈	6	7	8	9	10≈	11
12≈	13 FM	14	15	16	17	18
19	20	21	22	23	24	25
26	27	28	29	30		

2

					1≈	2≈
3	4	5	6	7	8	9
10	11	12	13	14≈	15≈	16
17≈	18	19	20≈ FM	21	22	23
24	25	26	27≈	28	29	30

5

					1≈	2
3≈	4	5	6	7≈	8	9
10≈	11	12	13	14	15	16
17 FM	18	19	20	21	22	23
24	25	26	27	28	29	30

8

					1	2
3	4	5	6	7	8	9
10	11	12	13	14	15≈ FM	16
17	18	19	20	21	22	23
24	25	26	27	28	29	30

11

					1≈	2
3	4	5	6	7	8	9
10	11	12 FM	13	14	15	16
17	18	19	20	21	22	23
24≈	25	26	27	28	29	30

3

1≈	2	3	4	5	6	7
8	9	10	11	12	13	14
15≈	16	17	18	19 FM	20	21
22	23≈	24	25	26	27	28
29	30	SS				

6

1≈	2	3	4	5≈	6	7
8	9	10	11	12	13	14
15	16	17 FM	18	19	20	21
22≈	23	24≈	25	26	27	28
29≈	30	AE				

9

1	2	3	4≈	5	6	7
8	9	10	11	12	13	14 FM
15	16	17	18	19	20≈	21
22	23	24≈	25	26	27	28
29	30	WS				

12

1≈	2	3≈	4	5	6	7
8	9	10	11	12 FM	13≈	14≈
15	16	17	18	19	20	21
22	23	24	25≈	26	27	28
29	30	SE				

Lunar Cycle 2
Hebrew Calendar Year _____
Qumran Calendar Rotation Number _____

Abib 1 — Moon Rise Time: _____ Moon Location _____

		1≈	2	3	4
5	6	7≈	8	9	10≈ 11 FM
12≈	13≈	14≈	15≈	16≈ 17	18
19	20	21≈ 22	23	24≈ 25	
26≈ 27	28	29	30		

2 — Moon Rise Time: _____ Moon Location _____

				1≈	2≈
3	4	5	6	7	8	9
10 FM	11	12	13	14≈ 15≈	16
17≈ 18	19	20≈ 21	22	23	
24	25	26	27≈ 28	29	30

3 — Moon Rise Time: _____ Moon Location _____

1≈	2	3	4	5	6	7
8	9 FM	10	11	12	13	14
15≈ 16	17	18	19	20	21	
22	23≈ 24	25	26	27	28	
29	30	SS				

4 — Moon Rise Time: _____ Moon Location _____

		1	2	3	4≈
5	6	7	8 FM	9≈ 10	11
12	13	14	15	16	17	18
19	20	21	22	23	24	25
26	27	28	29	30		

5 — Moon Rise Time: _____ Moon Location _____

				1≈	2
3≈ 4	5	6	7≈ 8 FM	9	
10≈ 11	12	13	14	15	16
17	18	19	20	21	22	23
24	25	26	27	28	29	30

6 — Moon Rise Time: _____ Moon Location _____

1≈	2	3	4	5≈ 6	7 FM
8	9	10	11	12	13	14
15	16	17	18	19	20	21
22≈ 23	24≈ 25	26	27	28	
29≈ 30	AE				

7 — Moon Rise Time: _____ Moon Location _____

		1≈	2	3	4
5 FM	6	7	8	9	10≈ 11
12	13	14	15≈ 16	17≈ 18	
19	20	21≈ 22≈ 23≈ 24	25		
26	27	28	29	30		

8 — Moon Rise Time: _____ Moon Location _____

				1	2
3	4	5 FM	6	7	8	9
10	11	12	13	14	15≈ 16	
17	18	19	20	21	22	23
24	25	26	27	28	29	30

9 — Moon Rise Time: _____ Moon Location _____

1	2	3	4≈ 5 FM	6	7
8	9	10	11	12	13	14
15	16	17	18	19	20≈ 21	
22	23	24≈ 25	26	27	28	
29	30	WS				

10 — Moon Rise Time: _____ Moon Location _____

		1	2	3	4 FM
5≈ 6	7	8	9	10≈ 11	
12≈ 13	14	15	16	17	18
19	20	21	22	23	24	25
26	27	28	29	30		

11 — Moon Rise Time: _____ Moon Location _____

				1≈	2 FM
3	4	5	6	7	8	9
10	11	12	13	14	15	16
17	18	19	20	21	22	23
24≈ 25	26	27	28	29	30	

12 — Moon Rise Time: _____ Moon Location _____

1≈	2 FM	3≈	4	5	6	7
8	9	10	11	12	13≈ 14≈	
15	16	17	18	19	20	21
22	23	24	25≈ 26	27	28	
29	30	SE				

Lunar Cycle 3
Hebrew Calendar Year _____
Qumran Calendar Rotation Number _____

Calendric Signs

Jubilee	1st Week of Years							2nd Week of Years							3rd Week of Years							4th Week of Years							5th Week of Years							6th Week of Years							Weeks of Release						
1	1	2	3	4	5	6	7	8	9	10	11	12	13	14	15	16	17	18	19	20	21	22	23	24	25	26	27	28	29	30	31	32	33	34	35	36	37	38	39	40	41	42	43	44	45	46	47	48	49
2	50	51	52	53	54	55	56	57	58	59	60	61	62	63	64	65	66	67	68	69	70	71	72	73	74	75	76	77	78	79	80	81	82	83	84	85	86	87	88	89	90	91	92	93	94	95	96	97	98
3	99	100	101	102	103	104	105	106	107	108	109	110	111	112	113	114	115	116	117	118	119	120	121	122	123	124	125	126	127	128	129	130	131	132	133	134	135	136	137	138	139	140	141	142	143	144	145	146	147
4	148	149	150	151	152	153	154	155	156	157	158	159	160	161	162	163	164	165	166	167	168	169	170	171	172	173	174	175	176	177	178	179	180	181	182	183	184	185	186	187	188	189	190	191	192	193	194	195	196
5	197	198	199	200	201	202	203	204	205	206	207	208	209	210	211	212	213	214	215	216	217	218	219	220	221	222	223	224	225	226	227	228	229	230	231	232	233	234	235	236	237	238	239	240	241	242	243	244	245
6	246	247	248	249	250	251	252	253	254	255	256	257	258	259	260	261	262	263	264	265	266	267	268	269	270	271	272	273	274	275	276	277	278	279	280	281	282	283	284	285	286	287	288	289	290	291	292	293	294

Key to Calendric Signs:* Highlighted Years represent use of first calendar cycle. *Every seven years a leap year occurs where seven days are added to the year, before the year begins. Leap years are indicated by colored numbers. By using "Daniel Moons" (86 moons +10 days = 3.5 years into 7 years tribulation) method of calculation year and assuming Christ was on Cross in AD 31 (cycle 1), the Gregorian calendar year 1941 used Calendric sign 147. In 1941 the Abib full moon was on Virgo's side.

From: http://www.haderech.info/DSS/Calendar/4Q319.pdf

Key to Qumran Calendar

KEY: FM = Full Moon; SS = Summer Solstice; AE = Autumn Equinox; WS = Winter Solstice; SE = Spring Equinox; Squiggle lines = Text from Bible Reference Date See Listed Month and Day

*****

Listed Times in the Bible. Feel free to observe holidays, observe signs and changes in the heavens and in nature according to what is written in the scripture. For more information on how the scripture is historically accurate and more proof is given to humanity since discovering the dead-sea scrolls visit www.kingscalendar.com, read the book of 'ENOCH' and study how the Qumran calendar operates. Example: The computer was used to search for specific dates in the bible. It was uncovered that on Abib 1 or the first month mentioned a little passage for the first day of the month in Genesis 8:13.

Note: This calendar is NOT "Hebrew roots" or "yahweist" movements. This is for information only and only contains computerized search tools to find specific dates mentioned. This calendar does not contain specific holidays, special times, feasts, events which are NOT discernible except by knowledge of Hebrew-Jewish culture and deeper study of the scripture ie. "feast of lights" or "Purim." An individual may use this as they feel helps them spiritually, or a church group may choose to follow the patterns from this calendar by observance of moon, sun and star heavenly signs. Those of higher intellectual capacity in a church group will have to assist those of lower intellectual capacity if the church group chooses to use this calendar to highlight certain days. Following a calendar does not SAVE a person from sin. Only faith and following Christ and his words keeps people from choosing sin. However, it can aide and help a person choose Christ over the world-system.

Abib -1 : Month mentioned (Num 9:1, Num 20:1, 1 Chr 12:15, 1 Chr 27:2, 1 Chr 27:3, 2 Chr 29:3, Joel 2:23) Day mentioned *1: Ezr 10:17, Ez 29:17, Ez 45:18, Gen 8:13, Ex 40:2, Ex 40:17, 2 Chr 29:17, Ezr 7:9 – *7: Ez 30:20 - *10: Josh 4:19 - *12: Ezr 8:31 - *13: Esth 3:92 - *14: Ex 12:18, Lev 23:5, Num 9:5, Num 28:16, 2 Chr 35:1, Ez 45:21 - *15: Num 33:3, 2 Chr 29:17, Ex 12:18, 2 Chr 29:17 - *16: 2 Chr 29:17 - *21: Ex 12:18 - *24: Dan 10:4

Iyyar – 2: Month mentioned (1 Kings 6:1, 1 Chr 27:4, 2 Chr 30:2, 2 Chr 30:13, Ez 3:8) Day mentioned *1: Num 1:1, Num 1:18 - *2: 2 Chr 3:2 - *14: Num 9:11, 2 Chr 30:15 - *15: Ex 16:1 - *17: Gen 7:11 - *20: Num 10:11 - *27: Gen 8:14

Sivan – 3: Month mentioned (Ex 19:1, 1 Chr 27:5, 2 Chr 15:10, 2 Chr 31:7) Day mentioned *1: Ezek 31:1 - *23: Esth 8:9

Tammuz – 4: Month mentioned (1 Chr 27:7, Jer 39:2, Zech 8:19) Day mentioned *5: Ez 1:1 - *9: 2 K 25:3, Jer 52:6

Ab – 5: Month mentioned (Ez 7:8, Jer 1:3, Jer 28:1, Zech 7:3) Day mentioned *1: Num 33:38, Ez 7:9 - *7: 2 K 25:8 - *10 Jer 52:12, Ez 20:1

Elul – 6: Month mentioned (1 Chr 27:9, Luke 1:26, Luke 1:36) Day mentioned *1: Hag 1:1 - *Ez 8:1 - *24: Hag 1:15

Tishri – 7: Month mentioned (Lev 23:41, 1 K 8:2, 2 K 25:25, 1 Chr 27:10, 2 Chr 5:3, 2 Chr 31:7, Ez 3:1, Neh 7:73, Neh 8:14, Jer 28:17, Jer 41:1, Zech 7:5) Day mentioned *1: Lev 23:24, Num 29:1, Ez 3:6, Neh 8:2 - *10: Lev 16: 29, Lev 23:27, Lev 25:9, Num 29:7 - *15: Lev 23:34, Lev 23:39, Num 29:12, Ez 45:25 - *17: Gen 8:4 - *21: Hag 2:1 - *2 Chr 7:10

Heshvan – 8: Month mentioned (1 K 6:38, 1 Chr 27:11, Zech 1:1) Day mentioned *15:1 K 12:32, 1 K 12:33

Chislev -9: Month mentioned (1 Chr 27:12, Jer 36:9, Jer 36:22) Day mentioned *4: Zech 7:1 - *20: Ez 10:9 - *24: Hagg 2:10, Hagg 2:18

Tebeth – 10: Month mentioned (1 Chr 27:13, Esth 2:16, Jer 39:1) Day mentioned *1: Gen 8:5, Ez 10:16 - *5: Ez 33: 21 - *10: 2 K 25:1, Jer 52:4, Ez 24:1 - *12: Ez 29:1

Shebat – 11: Month mentioned (1 Chr 27:14) Day mentioned *1: Deut 1:3 - *24: Zech 1:7

Adar – 12: Month mentioned (Esther 3:7) Day mentioned *1: Ezek 31:1 - *3: Ezra 6:15 - *13: Esther 3:13, Esth 8:12, Esth 9:1 - *14: Esth 9:19 - *25: Jer 52:31

No Servile Work Days: Lev:23:7 *1-14*, Lev 23:8 *1-21*, Lev 23:16 seven-Sabbaths or fifty days, Lev 23:24-25 *7-1*, Lev 23:27-28 *7-10*, *7-15* *7-23* Review Lev 23, Num 28, Num 29

Biblical Astronomy Conditions

Abib (spring constellations – Virgo: Naphtali, Libra: Dan, Scorpio:Simeon)

Iyyar (spring constellations - Virgo: Naphtali, Libra:Dan, Scorpio:Simeon)

Sivan (spring constellations - Virgo: Naphtali, Libra: Dan, Scorpio:Simeon)

Tammuz (Summer constellations – Sagitaurus: Gad, Capercorn:Reuben, Aquarius:Zebulun)

Ab (Summer constellations – Sagitaurus: Gad, Capercorn:Reuben, Aquarius:Zebulun)

Elul (Summer Constellations - Sagitaurus: Gad, Capercorn:Reuben, Aquarius:Zebulun)

Tishri (Fall Constellations – Pisces: Levi, Aeries: Issachar, Taurus: Asher)

Heshvan (Fall Constellations – Pisces: Levi, Aeries: Issachar, Taurus: Asher)

Chislev (Fall Constellations – Pisces: Levi, Aeries: Issachar, Taurus: Asher)

Tebeth(Winter Constellations – Gemini: Joseph, Cancer: Benjamin, Leo: Judah)

Shebat (Winter Constellations – Gemini: Joseph, Cancer: Benjamin, Leo: Judah)

Adar(Winter Constellations – Gemini: Joseph, Cancer: Benjamin, Leo: Judah)

Suggestion is to keep these months listed and the constellations listed as well in a poster form so that it is easier to understand.

The full moon will show up in and around the specific ecliptic constellations each season.

There are more details about biblical based astronomy from www.sonlighteducation.com , http://www.biblenews1.com/astrology/astrology.html and other resources. (the heavens declare the glory of God...but "stars" do not save people from sin life)

5. Numerical Calculations in Nature and in the Bible

0   Nothing   no reputation, think not of self

1   Beginning and Divine Unity   Light Darkness Aleph one savior, mighty, greater than Moses, grace and truth, above all gods, above all

2   Difference   Gasses/Liquid and Substance   Beth   full testimony, divine/human, good/evil, two lights(gen 1:16), two on the ark, two angels went to Sodom

3   Completeness Entireness   Plant Life   Gimel Three high powers (God, Son, Holy Spirit), Abe/Isaac/Jacob, Father/Mother/Child, Past/Present/Future, Liquid/Solid/Gas, omniscience/omnipresence/omnipotence, Orion, Clover leaves,

4 Creation Stars, Planets, Heavenly Bodies Daleth Earth/Fire/Air/Water, N-S-E-W, Evening/Midnight/Morning/Noon, four seasons, four types of lunar phases, four types of offerings in tabernacle, Tabernacle materials (3 metals, one wood), four chambers of the heart, coverings of tabernacle (3 animal, one linen(veg)), Four color ornamentation tabernacle (four color, one pattern)

5 Grace (five letters) Living Creatures He Five parts in Daniel 2, Five petaled flowers (ie. Almond), measurements in tabernacle multiple of 5, holy anointing oil 5 components, incense had five components, five fingers

6 man Man Vau man coming short of spiritual perfection, description of loaves and shewbread, Gen 18 intercede 6 times, Jesus charged 6 times (Mark 3:22; Matthew 12:24;John 7:20; John 8:48; John 8:52; John 10:20; and Luke 11:15), number 6 on great pyramids, 24 hour day divisible by 6, Cain's descendants lasted until 6th generation, lily flower has six petals,

7 Spiritual Perfection Rest Zayin seven occurs (7*41) times in old testament, seventy occurs 56 (7*8) times, golden candlestick 7 branches, seven days in a week, seven colors in rainbow, seven notes in musical scale, seven miracles by Jesus on Sabbath, clean animals on ark by sevens

8 New Beginning Chet seven main feasts and one more (Purim), eight lines out of persimmon flower, eight legs on spider,

eight people resurrected from dead in scripture, Jesus resurrected on 8th day, cubical measurements (2*2*2)...new Jerusalem is cubical,

9   Divine Completeness   Teth   Adam lived "nine" hundred years, parable with 99 sheep, Jesus cried at ninth hour, nine people stoned in bible, nine widows mentioned in the bible.

10   Completeness of Order   Yod   Noah was in 10th generation, 10 commandments, 10 clauses in Lord's Prayer, Abe faith tested 10 times, 10 times in Old Testament younger son preferred to older son, 10 toes in Daniel, 10 fingers, 10 symbolizes complete circle

11   Incompleteness   Yod Aleph   "11 dukes in Gen 36, Gen 42:32 one brother was not among 12, Deut 1:2 11 days journey, prophesied against Tyre and Egypt in 11th year (Ezekiel 26:1, 30:20, 31:1), 11 disciples after Jesus death, (Matthew 22:1-14; Luke 14:15-24; Matthew 20:1-16) 11th hour parables, "

12   Perfection in Government   Yod Beth   "12 sons of Jacob, 12 on breast plate, 12 cakes Leviticus 24:5-6, (I Kings 18:31-32) 12 stones, Jesus 12 years old mentioned (Luke 2:42), (Matthew 14:20) 12 baskets remained, 12's found in revelation, 2 lily flowers makes twelve petals, 12 months/constellations, New Jerusalem will be multiple of 12 (Revelation 21:16-17)"

Also consider that a certain number of "words" are used in scripture. The sound "sc" has 1480 matches and only certain "sc" words are presented. The word "scarlet" is presented 52 times. The word "leviathan" is mentioned 5 times.

ORDER OTHER MATERIALS by LAURA SPILDE

200 Day Biblical Classical Curriculum

Only 10$ for a complete curriculum educational material for elementary aged students.

(found on Amazon.com)

www.hens-and-chicks.blogspot.com

(free educational methods and materials guide)

Verity Files

An e-book with ramblings

(found on Amazon.com)

Kingdom Education

How to obtain a successful College Degree in the Liberal Arts with Bible Study emphasis, debt Free!

Major in a book of the bible instead of fruitless enterprises!

Are you tired of the headlines in today's news, which state that "College Tuition Rate is Increasing," "Christian Students Questioned for Their Faith," "Tax Increases 10 Times, Leaving Widows Homeless to Fund Free College," and "Massive College Debt Leaves Students Homeless after Graduating"? What about knowing that a terrorist, or a politically angry feminist actively obtained a bachelor degree from a Christian University while the poor repentant believer is denied an ability to speak at such a university? These things should not be in existence, as classical literature and history shows us that Christianity is the foundation of western thinking and morality and is the spiritual fruit for Eastern thinking! What about the feeling that a bible-believing Christian has neglected home and community for selfish pursuits, rather than real world experience and heartfelt change? Or what about cases of Christian hypocrisy when facing the trials of life, where if they only knew a better solution, they would not have made such poor choices? These problems do not have to be in existence. This book offers solutions to these problems, and more. Life is about celebrating independent thinking to rule out pride, to secure a true degree in the kingdom and in righteousness. Obtain such a degree without the hassles of debt and needless energy to study empty literature!

"The results of a liberal arts bible college degree, is not in the selfish pride of knowledge. It is in the overcoming of self, and willingness to serve others better out of the depth of our heart and the ability of Christ's strength within us. It is not to be used as a political force, but as a divine force of eternal love. " p. 159

Made in the USA
Lexington, KY
12 May 2018